UNLEASH EDUCATIONAL EXCELLENCE

Ensure Your Child's Success in School & Life

Revised Edition

Dr. Brenetia Adams-Robinson

Forward by Mary Hill-Hart, LPC, NCC, CPCS
(Clinical Counselor)

Endorsements by Elesha Curvey, MSW
(School Counselor)

UNLEASH EDUCATIONAL EXCELLENCE

Ensure Your Child's Success In School & Life

Dr. Brenetia Adams-Robinson

Forward

"Education is the passport to the future, for tomorrow belongs to those who prepare for it today." Malcolm X

Like Malcolm X, we understand the importance of what education represents for our future - the passport. One dictionary definition for Passport states, "a thing that ensures admission to or the achievement of something." Few books have had as great an impact on the need for academic collaboration between our parental figures and educators as Dr. Brenetia Adams-Robinson's *Unleash Educational Excellence*. This read drives home the truth about how family involvement in the educational process is what is required for our children across the world to be successful in their lifetime.

Dr. Adams-Robinson has gone back to the basics to ask one critical question: What am I doing to ensure my child's success in school and life? In doing so, she provides the secrets to master the strategy of educational success regardless of the related educational diversities. Providing quality education is important, but it is not going to help much if you don't take charge and start at home with your children!

Everyone needs education. Everyone needs a supportive environment. Everyone needs a reminder that they are not alone in the academic process. Everyone needs the confidence to know they are destined to do amazing things. If we don't grasp these things, our children simply will not learn, and there is nothing much our educators or any academic institution can do about it. Dr. Adam-Robinson is sounding the alarm bells and bringing this to our attention as she so poignantly shares her journey as a parent with three very different children who required separate, individualized academic approaches.

We all can do something about this academic dilemma, and it does not require a scholar. We can do something about this right now, starting in our own homes by engaging in the homework process. You must take responsibility for your children and work closely with our academic partners to get the educational success you need. And you must take a leap of faith and look inside your own four walls.

This book shows you several ways to make instant changes in your children's lives if you are willing to try. May each reader continue to use this book as a resource while serving those beginning their didactical journey. It is my prayer, **Unleash Educational Excellence** will motivate you to seek a new way that you and your family can raise confident, smart, intelligent children destined to do great things!

Mary Hill Hart, LPC, NCC, CPCS
Founder/CEO
HART Recovery Center, LLC

Endorsement

As a school social worker and a parent, I am so excited about this new resource guide, *Unleash Educational Excellence*! This book has taken parent involvement to the next level by providing user-friendly strategies that will empower parents and students from Kindergarten through High School. It also helps parents to remove barriers that potentially cause educational apathy, low grades, poor attendance, and low self-esteem.

You will find that after utilizing the practical step-by-step tools provided for various educational barriers and issues, a child's trajectory for future success is inevitable. This book will become the next must-read resource guide for not only parents but also teachers, school social workers, guidance counselors, and other school support staff.

Elesha R. Curvey, MSW
School Social Worker
Atlanta Public Schools

Table of Content

Preface

A child educated only at school is an uneducated child.

Families play a vital role in educating children. Parental influence is proven to be more important to student success in school than any other impact concerning the family dynamic. This is true whether the children are in elementary, junior high, or high school. Research studies support the direct link between parental involvement and how children perform in school and how seriously they take their educational journey.

Educational research consistently supports that children who master homework strategies do better in school than children who do not. It is the influence of the parent or other parental/guardian figure in the home that determines how a child views education, learning, homework, and school interactions.

Helping your child embrace learning and mastering homework strategies does not mean that you must be an expert at the subject the child is studying, nor even be highly educated yourself. Indeed, your involvement does not necessitate you knowing anything about the subject matter at all. It does, however, mandate that you show your child how important school and homework is to you as a parent or parental figure. You must positively show them that their success as students is of vital concern to you.

Unleash Educational Excellence is an invaluable and practical resource guide to help parents and the family support system become more actively involved in their children's learning process and to better assist students in doing the critical work to achieve academic success. It provides step-by-step information and strategies to ensure you help position your child for success in the school year and beyond.

The value of mastering the learning process and homework strategies extends beyond school. We know that effective assignments completed successfully can help children develop wholesome habits and attitudes that will serve them throughout their lives. Taking part in the homework process can help parents learn about what's going on in their child's education; shed light and understanding of what's going on in their child's mind about their experiences, and enhance communication with both their child and the school. This participatory process can encourage a lifelong love of learning under-girded by feelings of enhanced self-confidence in a child's ability to learn and achieve whatever goals they desire in life.

Additionally, parents can help their children in the learning process by encouraging them to spend more leisure time reading than watching television. They can talk with their child and communicate positive behaviors and values. Parental participation promotes and encourages a more open dialogue between the parent, the teacher, and the school, which sends a strong message to the child that the educational journey is critically important, and success is not only your desire but your expectation.

Connect for Success

The information in this invaluable manual will help parents face the challenges of raising children in today's difficult child-rearing climate and taking them one step closer to life-long success. You owe it to your child to help them achieve the greatness that is within them. You owe it to you and your family to be a part of such a wonderful journey!

The Success Equation

Original Unknown / Adapted by Dr. B. Adams-Robinson

I dreamt I stood in a creative space,
and watched two artists there.
The clay they used was a young child's mind
which they fashioned with tender care.

One was a teacher, the tools that were used
were books, paper, music, and art.
One was a parent with a guiding hand
and a gentle and loving heart.

Day after day, the teacher toiled
with a touch that was skillful and firm.
While the parent labored with encouraging words,
and ensured home learning was norm.

And when, in the end, their work was done,
they were proud of what they had wrought.
For the things they molded in the young child's mind,
could neither be sold nor be bought.

Each quickly agreed that they would have failed
if they had each worked all alone.
For behind every parent stands a committed teacher,
and behind every teacher, the home.

When parents and teachers commit to the child
to always work side by side.
The child reaps the rewards of wondrous things,
and their greatness unfolds and resides.

CHAPTER 1
PARENT-CHILD RELATIONSHIP
~THE CRITICAL EDGE~

"Train up a child in the way he should go, and even when he is old he will not depart from it." Proverbs 22:6

As a young child of 7 years of age, I experienced one of the most devastating things a child can experience - my mother was killed in a car crash. She died instantly. The other five people in the vehicle survived but were severely injured. My father had long since abandoned us. So, my mother was the only parent I had, and she made me feel like a little princess every day. But in an instant, she was gone. Blessedly, my maternal grandmother accepted the challenge of raising me. Because she was in her mid-70's at the time, she engaged the assistance of her youngest daughter, my youngest aunt, to help her with my upbringing.

My grandmother was illiterate and had never learned to read or write. So, she didn't really understand the alpha-numeric system. She would have my aunt explain what was on my report card; as a result, she knew the impact of an 'A' versus a 'C' (D and F were not even allowed in the vocabulary of my house ☺). Because she could not read or write, she instilled in me the need to do well in school, the need to finish school, and the desire to embrace every opportunity to learn and grow. My aunt was not a scholarly student in school. As she would always say, she 'C'd' her way through school and was happy to see those C's. But she reinforced my grandmother's message and expectations of doing well in school... and she had a pipeline to key connections in my school.

1

She had a long-standing friendship with the school counselor and knew several of the administrators. Unknown to me, she had each of them watching out for me. She had instructed them to let her know if and when anything occurred that they felt needed to be addressed, and to let her know of opportunities that I could or should be involved in. I was extremely shy and introverted, so I would seldom volunteer to participate in anything without prompting. But with my aunt's connections, even when I did not have the confidence to ask about something or to boldly volunteer when a school event was upcoming, administrators and teachers would come to me and encourage me to participate. In several instances, I was volun-told that I would participate.

Next to my aunt, my grandmother was my biggest cheerleader. Her encouragement led me to embrace a desire to excel in school, and to want to take advantage of all possible educational opportunities. My aunt's behind-the-scene active participation in my school journey kept me on a path of success, such that failure was not an option. With the two of them in my corner, quitting was not an option and failure a foreign language.

With my mother's death, my biological father's abandonment, and some of the traumas that followed, I could have easily been a statistic. However, because of my grandmother's and aunt's interest and participation in my educational journey, I graduated top two of my high school class, honors graduate in college, and obtained my doctorate (an achievement that only 3% of the nation ever obtains). These 2 major influences in my life were not scholars or highly educated. But because they planted seeds of encouragement and motivation within me, I am an avid reader and lifelong learner. They had no concept of college life, and neither were here to see me achieve my doctorate. However, because of the seeds they planted, even in their absence, their silent voices of encouragement and inspiration kept me moving to achieve greater.

Education and learning are the cornerstone of success and must be cultivated early in every child to position them to be the best that they can be. The planting of those seeds and the watering process starts at home. The pandemic brought about a major shift in the entire framework of education around the world. Prior to this terrible crisis, most parents conceived the educational process as completely the teacher's job. The pandemic re-iterated a fundamental truth – the educational journey must be a collaborative joint venture with parents and educators work together if the child will have every possible opportunity to succeed.

During the early stages of this worldwide health crisis, the separation, sheltering in place, and isolation forced parents to assume the semi-role of educator. Teachers gave lessons online while parents had to monitor the child to ensure they stayed engaged in a virtual platform most had never encountered. Parents had to quickly develop sufficient support skills to assist teachers to ensure students 'get' the lessons that were being assigned and to ensure students don't get severely behind in their studies. To most parents this was a terrifying, unsettling, and frustrating endeavor; but successfully fulfilling the role was imperative.

I am not a child psychologist, but my experiences as a parent, busy professional, community advocate, and child advocate have taught me so many lessons that we, as parents, must know to be able to position our children for long-term success. As a busy, working parent, I know how hard it is to have to make time for children after long, non-stop days. As a parent of three very different children, I had to learn to work with very diverse school systems, diverse teaching strategies, and sometimes very complicated school situations. As an ex-military spouse, I have worked collaboratively with school systems in the overseas community and in the U.S.

As a divorced parent, I had to master the strategy of being a single parent working with my kids' teachers and keeping my ex-husband (non-resident father) actively connected to that process. As the parent of a special needs child, I had to maneuver through the sometimes difficult process of understanding the importance of parents and teachers working together for the good of my child while accommodating the special need. As an employee who worked in a leadership capacity in a state family services agency, I understand the nuances of the foster care system and the challenges of foster care parenting. Through all of these experiences, I have seen successes and endured flat-out failures on the parenting journey that taught some hard-earned lessons.

Needless to say, I know first-hand how absolutely critical it is for parents and families to support a child and undergird his or her capacity for success; and how crucial it is for parents to embrace educators as close family friends. Now, I reiterate, I've made some glaring mistakes as a parent and had to embrace some hard lessons. But I've also realized that as parents, mistakes are part of the journey. It's what you do with the mistakes that makes the difference between parental success and failure. Parental mistakes do not take away from your influence over your child - you are still the most powerful individual in your child's life and on your child's path to success. But that path starts with a strong educational foundation. This resource is purposed to provide strategies to ensure that, as a parent, you know how to make that happen.

4

Research over the last 20 years supports that there is a direct link between family involvement in the education process at all ages, and a child's overall success to include educationally, socially, and in goal setting. The impact of the pandemic has supported past research findings that parental involvement in the educational process is a more significant factor in a child's academic success than the qualities of the school itself. This means that a child can attend a poorly ranked school, but still be greatly successful if the primary parent is actively involved in the child's educational journey. Some factors cited as the most impactful on the educational success journey include the family structure, parental involvement, and the child's focus on educational importance.

The Research Speaks

Studies reveal that parental involvement in schools tends to decrease as children move from elementary to middle to high school. This suggests that parents have the misbelief that younger children need more parental support than older children; and that as children get older, there is less need for parental involvement as they exert their need for independence. Studies also support that two-parent households tend to be more involved than single-parent families.

This dynamic is due to two primary factors. First, with two parents in the home, the greater the likelihood that one parent will be readily available to the child when needed. Second, a single parent has limited time to commit to a child when they have to maintain a home single-handedly. This points to the fact that single parents have to be more strategic and intentional about their involvement with the child's educational journey.

Studies have also found that the greater a parent's education and socioeconomic status, the more they tend to be involved in the educational process. This is likely because less-educated parents tend to feel more intimidated by the school setting, the homework process, and interacting with a child's teachers and administrators. This can lead to parents with less education believing that their involvement is not critical or that there is little value that they can lend to the child's educational process.

Every study or family-based research obviously supports that this is not true. Regardless of a parent's education level or socioeconomic position, a child needs his or her parent to be engaged at every stage of the educational process to help the child be the best that they can be when it comes to their education journey. Some studies focus primarily on a mother's influence when it comes to single-parent homes because mothers tend to be the primary caregivers.

Mothers who work full-time and those in the job search process (which can be an all-consuming process) tend to be less involved in school activities than mothers who work part-time. This is linked directly to the time factor. In the immediacy, the time needed to ensure the family's financial well-being takes on a greater priority than the need to be active in the educational process. Although paying the bills is critical and necessary, it is short-sighted because the message to the child is that the educational process is not that important. It is even more critical that parents in this situation are intentional and strategic about the message that they communicate to their child in this regard.

Other factors that influence the level of parental involvement include how confident the parent is that the child can do well in school; if they have high educational aspirations for the child; and the school's policies and practices. Despite the various reasons that explain why parents might not engage in a child's learning, prudent parents must be intentional in staying connected to what is going on with the child in school and the educational process at large. This is the only way to ensure a child's path to educational and life-long success.

When families, especially parents, are involved in a child's education, the overall educational performance is greatly increased and has much higher returns than students of parents who are not involved. Therefore, it is critical for families to be intricately involved in the educational process.

Anne Henderson and Nancy Berla are noted educational researchers who have done exhaustive research concerning the link between a child's education and the support they get at home as well as the correlation between a family's involvement with a child's school. After reviewing and assessing more than 100 research studies, Henderson and Berla have deemed that the most accurate predictor of a student's success in school is not based on income or social status; but is directly related to a family's capacity to facilitate the following:

1. Create a home environment that encourages a student's success in learning.

2. Express high (but not unrealistic) expectations for their children's educational achievements, as well as for future goals and objectives.

3. Become involved in their children's education at school and in the community.

According to research by Southwest Educational Development Laboratory, a collaborative of researchers who study parental involvement in education, when schools, families, and community groups work together to support a child's education and learning, children are consistently more successful than in environments where education is not a primary focus of support.

Parental Involvement Benefits

The family of giant sequoia trees holds the record for the largest and tallest trees in the world. They can live an average of 3,000 years, have branches up to 8 feet in diameter, have barks that grow up to 3 feet thick, and have grown as high as an average of a 26-story building. These amazing trees spread out to 35 feet in width. It would take six people laid out head-to-toe to match this width. These trees are hardy enough to resists fungal attacks, beetle attacks, and fires; things that have been known to destroy other trees.

These amazing creations are almost indestructible. If each sequoia produced on only one seed in its lifetime, the sequoia trees would never become extinct, because that one seed will produce a tree that will last thousands of years. One sequoia seed is saturated with greatness. Like the sequoia, every child is born with a seed of greatness inside them. Every child is a God-made masterpiece, designed for a unique purpose with extraordinary gifts and talents to pursue purpose, despite any negative circumstances of their birth.

Every child deserves appropriate support, encouragement, and a chance to make their dreams their reality, despite the environment in which they live. Every child deserves a joyous, happy, fulfilling life – it's their promise from God. What they go through in their young lives will determine if that seed of promise becomes a poisonous plant, laddened with destruction and bitterness; or whether they will grow into a giant sequoia, capable of becoming the great entity they were meant to be. How you nurture the seed within your child provides the care and nourishment that the seed needs for glorious growth.

Numerous research findings support that children need to hear and feel that their parent(s) think they can achieve and succeed. That's when the seed of greatness is watered and can flourish. I've witnessed many parents who just assume that the child just 'knows' what parents think and feel about the child's abilities. However, in order for a child to truly believe that they can be great, parents must consistently water the seed within them to grow into their greatness. A child needs to **hear** words of support and validation in order to **be** encouraged and inspired to be successful.

When parents talk to their children about school, expect them to do well, make sure that out-of-school activities are constructive, and help them plan for college, children perform much better in school and actively seek to reach the expectations of the parental figure. Parents must be vocal about their desires and expectations for their child to ensure the child believes they can do and be what parents tell them they can be.

Family support of children and school activities promote benefits for children, parents, educators, and schools.

Benefits for the Children:

- ❖ Children with a strong family support system are more successful in school as well as with extracurricular and community activities regardless of ethnic or racial background, socioeconomic status, or parents' education level.

9

❖ They achieve better grades, higher test scores, and better attendance.

❖ They consistently complete their homework successfully; and are more vocal in the classroom as a result of the stronger foundation of confidence.

❖ They have more self-esteem, are more self-disciplined, and show higher aspirations and motivation in both goals related to activities in school and outside of the school.

❖ They have better social skills and adapt well to various situations. This leads to more positive interactions with other students as well as with their teachers.

❖ They have a more positive attitude about school, resulting in better behavior, less negative responses, and fewer disciplinary issues. This leads to more successful engagement in other areas of interest, as well.

❖ They have less likelihood of being placed in special education and remedial classes unless there are actual needs based on physical or mental limitations.

❖ They are more likely to graduate and go on to postsecondary education.

❖ They have a much higher possibility of overall success after graduation.

Benefits for the Parents:

❖ Engaged and involved parents have increased interactions, discussion, and dialogue with their children about all areas of life, not just school-related issues.

❖ They tend to be more responsive and sensitive to their children's social, emotional, and intellectual developmental needs.

- They are more confident in their parenting and capacity to make sound decisions.

- They are more knowledgeable about child development, which results in more use of affection and positive reinforcement, and less punishment on their children.

- They are more aware of what the learning process entails, which increases the likelihood of being able to help when teachers need parental assistance, and more readily involved with homework.

- They have more positive perceptions, stronger ties, and more commitment to the school and school personnel.

- They are more aware of (and become more active regarding) policies that affect their children's education.

- They have a better understanding of the teacher's job and school curriculum.

Benefits for the Educators:

- When schools have a high percentage of involved parents in schools, teachers and principals are more likely to experience higher morale.

- Teachers and principals often earn greater respect for their profession from the parents.

- Consistent parental and family unit involvement leads to improved communication and relations between parents, teachers, and administrators.

- Teachers and principals acquire a better understanding of families' cultures and diversity dynamics, and they form deeper respect for parents' abilities and time.

❖ Teachers are better equipped to help each student based on their knowledge of the unique needs of each student to maximize learning.

❖ Teachers and principals report an increase in job satisfaction.

Benefits for the School:

❖ Schools that actively involve parents and the community in educational activities tend to have better reputations in the community.

❖ Schools with active parental involvement experience better community support.

❖ School programs that encourage and involve parents usually do better and have higher quality programs than those that do not involve parents.

Henderson and Berla ultimately assessed that the evidence is Indisputable. When families support student learning and the educational process, children tend to succeed not just in school, but throughout life. Junior high and high school students whose families remain involved throughout the school experience make better transitions to higher grade levels, are less likely to drop out of school, and are more likely to seek post-secondary avenues to achieve success in life.

The chart below outlines why many parents say they cannot help their children with homework or otherwise make excuses for not being actively involved in the educational process.

Why HALF of U.S. Parents Can't Help Their Kids with Homework

5 out of 10 parents say they have trouble helping their children with homework.

Why do so many parents fear they are falling short? Of those who have trouble...

21.9%
ARE TOO BUSY

31.6%
SAY THEIR KIDS DON'T WANT THEIR HELP

46.5%
DON'T UNDERSTAND THE MATERIAL

www.famlit.org

Do not let your child fall into a statistic. Do not let your doubts, fears, and time management keep your child from the glorious potential and promise God has given them. Help them tap into their greatness. They need you to make that happen; it starts at home.

CHAPTER 2
HOMEWORK - HITTING THE MARK

"However, you help your child with homework, don't lose sight of whose assignment it really is." Unknown

Why Is Homework Important?

Homework is meant to be a positive experience and to encourage children to learn and grow, and should never be connected to punishment in the mind of a child. To do so does homework a negative aspect of school rather than something that should be deemed as a positive aspect of the educational journey. Homework is purposed to help your child understand critical learning elements, make assignments more meaningful, and help your child complete assignments successfully. Homework assignments generally always have a specific purpose, should come with clear instructions from the teacher, be well matched to a student's grade and abilities, and be designed to help develop a student's knowledge and skills in a specific subject matter.

In the early elementary grades, homework assignments are simplistic, purposed to help children develop the habits and attitudes needed to lay a foundation for continued educational success. From fourth through sixth grades, homework assignments will gradually increase each year, supporting stronger cognitive abilities to improve academic achievement.

As a child progresses, homework becomes more complex to help a child increase critical thinking and problem-solving skills. Research supports that students in 7th grade and beyond who complete homework assignments successfully score better on standardized tests and earn better grades than

14

students who do less homework. Successful homework strategies promote more confidence in students when it comes to class participation as well as in overall school interactions.

According to a report developed by the U.S. Department of Education, research strongly supports that there are specific strategies related to homework that must be employed to lay a foundation for success on a child's educational journey.

Homework, properly monitored, have the following benefits:

- ❖ It can improve remembering and understanding of schoolwork.
- ❖ It helps students develop study skills that will be of value even after they leave school.
- ❖ It teaches students that learning takes place anywhere, not just in the classroom.
- ❖ It fosters positive character traits, such as independence and responsibility.
- ❖ It teaches children how to manage time.

If not properly monitored, homework can have some negative consequences that parents must be consistently mindful of:

- ❖ Students will grow bored or extremely fatigued if they are required to spend too much time on schoolwork after a full day of school.
- ❖ Too much homework can prevent children from taking part in leisure or community activities that also teach important life skills.
- ❖ Collaborative homework assignments may lateral into cheating.

How Much Homework is Enough?

Educational professionals and experts agree that the amount

of homework should depend on the age and skills of the child. Studies on effective homework strategies suggest that homework should follow the general rules below:

- ❖ For children in kindergarten through second grade, homework time should not exceed 10-20 minutes each day, emphasizing that shorter and more frequent assignments are more effective than longer periods.
  - This is because young children have a shorter span of attention, which is critical to them achieving a sense of accomplishment in completing a given task.
- ❖ In third through sixth grade, children benefit most from 30-60 minutes of homework per day.
- ❖ Junior high and high school students can benefit from more time on

  homework, and the amount may vary from night to night.
- ❖ Reading at home is especially important for young children.

Types of Homework:

Homework assignments typically have one or more purposes. The most common purpose is to have students practice material already presented in class.

- ❖ **Practice homework** reinforces learning and helps the student master specific skills that were introduced in the classroom.
- ❖ **Preparation homework** introduces material that will be presented in future lessons to help students learn new material better when it is covered in class.
- ❖ **Extension homework** asks students to apply skills they already have or have mastered to new situations.

❖ **Integration homework** requires the student to apply many different skills to a single task, such as book reports, science projects, or creative writing.

Math homework has been shown to be more important in the middle to high school grades and less important in the elementary grades. It starts to become important in the fourth grade and is increasingly important in the upper grades.

The Parental Involvement Paradigm

Children need to know that parents and close family members believe that homework is important. When parents show they care and are committed to active participation, children are motivated to complete assignments and turn them in on time. There is a lot that you can do to show that you value education and homework.

Research shows that parental involvement is essential to how a student perceives the value of homework on their educational journey. It is important that parents are intentional in how they participate in supporting a child in their education process. The parental involvement process can have positive and negative impacts on a child's homework experience.

When done properly, parental involvement has the following advantageous benefits:

❖ It can be used to enhance a child's learning of the material that is studied.

❖ Can improve the parent's engagement in the school process.

❖ Can enhance a parent's appreciation of the educational process as well as parent-teacher relationships.

- ❖ Can improve communication between the school, the teacher, and the family.
- ❖ Can better help parents understand what is expected of students.
- ❖ Can give parents a firsthand idea of what students are learning and how well their child is doing in school.

Avoid Negative Parenting Possibilities

Parental involvement can also have negative influences on the learning process if not managed properly:

- ❖ Parents can confuse children if their teaching style differs from the child's teacher's style.
  - Parents should talk to teachers to ask for advice based on what is being done in the classroom.
- ❖ Involvement can become interference if the parent begins to complete tasks for the child or give answers to questions.
  - This will undermine the student's capacity to use their brains in solving homework tasks and may lead to laziness in the learning process.
- ❖ Becoming impatient, argumentative, and frustrated with the child will lead to a child equating education with trauma, which will only lead to more difficulties in all future learning activities.
  - They will begin to dislike school or learning. Rather than becoming impatient, parents should encourage the child to take a break and relax.
  - If they continue to struggle, the parents must connect with the child's teacher to work collaboratively to determine how best to help the child succeed.

18

- If parents find that a child is struggling with homework assignments, they must be patient and supportive of the child's struggles. By exhibiting patience and continuous encouragement, you are sending the message that you believe in your child's ability to do what is expected, and you are committed to helping them reach the goal.

To reduce or eliminate the potential for the negative and increase the positive benefits, it is important that parents keep the best interest of the child in mind with every decision and every educational contact. Being actively involved in the child's educational process is not about how the parent looks or feels, it's about doing what's in the best interest of the child to enhance their potential for long term success in life. Positive parental participation is critical to make that happen. If a child is doing well in school, it in no way means that a parent is to leave the child to his or her own devices.

Parenting the Natural Born Student

If you are blessed with a child who has natural educational talents, rather than leave them to complete their homework on their own, that is the time for parents to encourage the child to think outside the box and expand learning outside of just what is assigned. This situation, too, could be an opportunity for both parent and teacher to collaborate to ensure the child does not become bored and is positioned to be maximally successful.

General Homework Tips

Now that there is a clear understanding of the importance of homework, and of parental figures laying the right foundation for homework success, it is important to outline the tactical strategies to create a strong learning environment to ensure children are successful in homework assignments. Below are guidelines for creating a learning environment in the home.

The Environment

❖ Make sure your child has a quiet, well-lit place to do homework. If possible, your child may enjoy decorating their study area to make it their own, i.e., a brightly colored container for pencils, favorite artwork, etc.

❖ Avoid having your child do homework with the television on or in places with other distractions, such as people coming and going.

❖ If you live in a small or noisy household, consider making homework time a family-focused time to ensure your child's success.

- One idea is to have a 'homework spot' where all children sit in the room together to do homework. Then parents can check on everyone at one time and offer help where needed. This will truly impress upon the children that education is a number one priority for the family.

- Try having all family members take part in a quiet activity before homework to calm everyone down and quiet the atmosphere.

The Resources

❖ Make sure the materials your child needs, such as paper, pencils, and a dictionary, are available.

- If there are financial hindrances to providing needed supplies, check with the teacher, school guidance counselor, or principal about possible sources of assistance.

- For books and other information resources, check with the school library or local public library. Some libraries have homework centers designed specially to assist children with school assignments.

❖ Ask your child if special materials will be needed for some projects and get them in advance.

Time Management

❖ Help your child with time management. Establish a set time each day for doing homework. An older student can probably make up a schedule independently, although you'll want to make sure it's a good one.

❖ Don't let your child leave homework until just before bedtime. This will only produce frustration in everyone while rushing to get it all done on time.

❖ Think about using a weekend morning or afternoon to work on big projects, especially if the project involves getting together with classmates.

Your Involvement

❖ Be positive about homework. Tell your child how important school is. The attitude you express about homework will be the attitude your child acquires.

❖ When your child does homework, you do homework. Show your child that the skills they are learning are related to things you do as an adult. If your child is reading, you read too. If your child is doing math, balance your checkbook.

❖ When your child asks for help, provide guidance, not answers. Giving answers means your child will not learn the material. Too much help teaches your child that when the going gets rough, someone will do the work for them. This will only lead to an entitlement attitude that will last into adulthood and will not build a foundation of accountability nor a strong work ethic.

❖ When the teacher asks that you play a role in homework, do it. Cooperate with the teacher. It shows your child that school and home are a team. Follow the directions given by the teacher. Remember, just as you have expertise in your work, the teacher is a specialist at what she does.

❖ Stay informed. Talk with your child's teacher. Make sure you know the purpose of homework assignments and what your child's class rules are.

❖ Help your child figure out what is hard homework and what is easy homework. Have your child do the hard work first. This will mean he will be most alert when facing the biggest challenges. Easy material will seem to go fast when fatigue begins to set in.

A Positive Homework Experience

When you create a learning environment in your home, it is important that you are an active participant in your child's learning process. Of course, it will be easier if you have knowledge of what your child is studying. However, it **IS NOT** mandatory. You don't have to know the topic being studied. You just have to be present, show your interest in your child's homework process, and actively encourage your child to do his or her best.

Watch for Fatigue and Frustration

❖ Monitor your child for signs of fatigue, irritation, and frustration. Let your child take a short break if there is trouble focusing on an assignment.

- Ask them what the source of their frustration and irritation is.

- If it does not appear that they will be able to figure things out, and you are not knowledgeable on the subject, take note so that you can send the teacher an email for younger children.

❖ For older children, instruct them to talk to the teacher, then make sure you follow up to ensure they connected to the teacher to ask the necessary questions.

Make Success Special

❖ Reward successful outcomes in difficult or large homework projects and assignments.

- If your child has been successful in homework completion of large or difficult projects or assignments, celebrate that success with a special event or celebration (e.g., family pizza party, time together outside, a trip to the park, a special family dinner) to reinforce the positive effort and outcome.

- The celebration does not have to be on the same day. You can let your child know that something fun is coming on the weekend, or on payday. This will add excitement to the week and give them something exciting to look forward to.

- Depending on what you plan or can afford, add to the excitement by letting them participate in the planning.

Make the Library Family Friendly

❖ Make time to take your child to the library when they need library materials for homework. Don't just drop them off and leave.

- When possible, join them. You will be surprised what you can find of interest in the library while they do what they have to do.

- This can also be a wonderful opportunity to learn and grow with your child if it is a subject or area of which you have no or limited knowledge.

- Growing with your child is a phenomenal way to deepen your relationship and build a stronger bond with your child. Parents often feel embarrassed if their child is studying a topic they don't know. They sometimes feel the child may not respect them or honor them if they know the parent lacks certain knowledge. However, children see things differently. By being willing to grow and learn with them, you are teaching them never to stop their own growing process, all while you bond and strengthen the relationship with them.

Library Family Outings

❖ Library visits don't have to be just for homework. This is another opportunity for a family-focused activity to impress upon your child that 'reading is FUNdamental,' and encourage your child to develop strong reading skills.

- For younger children, let them choose a book to check out and make

  time to read with them as often as you can.

- For older children, especially teens, let them choose a book that you both check out, read, and discuss. This is a very strategic, yet non-meddling way to hear how your child thinks about different topics and how they see different scenarios.

Stay Actively Engaged

❖ Talk about school and learning activities in family conversations. Ask your child what was discussed in class that day. If they don't have much to say, try another approach to get them talking about school to show how interested you are.

❖ Attend school activities, such as parent-teacher conferences or sports events. Volunteer to help with school events when possible.

❖ Get to know some other parents and their children to build a network of support for you and your child.

Home-Learning Success

Setting a regular regimen for homework and creating the right space to do assigned homework tasks is foundational to creating the expectations of how important you view education. As a parent, you set the tone for your child's mindset concerning education, and your actions tell your child how seriously his or her educational journey is to you. You set that expectation with loving words, encouraging actions, and consistency. When you create an environment in the home conducive to educational excellence, then learning is an easy task and a much more desirable path for your child.

You must create the culture of learning in your home to ensure your child's success. An effective Home-Learning Culture mandates a unified focus on a strong foundation of parental encouragement, consistent parental involvement at home and at school, and basic resources to complete assignments. When these components are a constant in the home, the child will be positioned for educational success in any situation.

CHAPTER 3
HOMEWORK SUCCESS STRATEGIES

"As a parent, trust yourself. You know more than you think you do."
Benjamin Spock

Research related to understanding the best strategies to enhance the homework learning process supports that children are more likely to complete assignments successfully when parents monitor homework. With the busy schedules that drive most households in today's fast-paced climate, it is easy to allow life's pace to interfere with the homework monitoring process. However, it is just important for parents to plan this process in the family's daily routine as it is to prepare for dinner and other end of the day activities. One of the hindrances to the process is the fact that not all families have positive family routines.

Significance of Family Routines

A routine is defined as a sequence of actions regularly followed or a fixed program within a system. Even when it is not consciously known, all families operate in routines as a foundation of what is normal in the family structure, that is, a way the family gets things done. Children are even more prone to operate best when they have a normal routine to follow. A normal routine brings comfort and consistency to a child's life.

Some daily routines include the process they follow to get ready for school each morning, homework guidelines, bath time, mealtime, weekend house cleaning, etc. Routines provide a normal framework for children to function and lets them know what's important to you and to the family. Those things then become important to them. Routines are important to a child's development because of the following:

1. Consistent routine influences a child's internal 'body clock' concerning daily basics such as:

   - For babies and young children: nap time and nightly sleeping schedules, which becomes a norm as they will begin to wind down when it's bedtime.
   - Mealtimes and healthy eating habits.
   - Healthy play routines, which lay the foundation of how they interact as they grow.
   - Getting up and getting prepared for their daily activities.

   When the family dynamic does not involve these basic routines, nap and bedtime become mini battles; eating habits veer to the unhealthy; relationships may be contentious; and preparation for school becomes chaos.

2. Family routines increase family unity and bond family members in common goals. When children know and understand the expectations of family members in regular activities, they will begin to embrace the concepts of what's important to the family, which strengthens family values. Family routines bond family members together and are unspoken statements of what values the family believes are important. Children will embrace those routines and values.

3. Routines establish expectations and make it easier for children to understand what they are supposed to do. Rather than bath time or chore time being a power struggle, establishing a routine helps a child get acclimated

to their role in the family, and expectations will become their 'normal.' As a result, children will begin to complete the chores, go to bed, do what's expected without issues, without argument, and with minimum stress. This will make for a stronger family bond, a calmer household, and more successful family outcomes.

4. Established routines give your child confidence and enhances their foundation of independence. When positive and consistent routines are established in a home, the child learns and willingly embraces a normal morning routine of getting ready for school, understands how the family views homework processes, follows the 'rules' of respect for others, and have constructive interactions with others. Rather than being told what needs to happen, your child will just do it. They will take pride in doing what they are supposed to do, feel good about themselves when they are successful in doing what's expected and are less likely to rebel or retaliate.

5. Having positive, established routines help children cope during times of change or stress. Although, as adults, we know that change is constant in life, children don't like change and are generally stressed by changes that impact their world, i.e., divorce, changing schools, merging families, negative family traumas, etc. When normal family routines remain consistent, a child has some sense of 'normal' in his or her life. Although there is a major change, they can still hold on to some things that make sense to them.

6. Routines help to minimize arguments or lengthy discussions trying to get your child to do what's expected because, with routines in place, expectations become a part

28

of a child's normal behavior. You may initially deal with whys and resistance, but consistency leads to what will become routine. When children understand the consequences of inappropriate behaviors, bickering and adverse responses will be greatly lessened, and threats of discipline will reduce as well.

The Importance of Family Routines

According to the American Academy of Pediatrics, a strong family needs family routines. They help to organize a family's interactions and keep things from becoming chaotic, disorganized, and unduly hectic. Children do best when family routines are consistent, predictable, and reliable. No structure results in family chaos; too much structure results in inflexibility and no fun. One of the greatest challenges for parents is establishing effective routines that help achieve a happy compromise between the disorder and confusion of no routines and the rigidity and boredom that can come with too much structure.

The American Academy of Pediatrics suggests incorporating some of the following ideas in developing family routines:

Weekday Mornings:

Establish morning routines that make it easier to get everyone up and out the door.

❖ Prepare as much as possible at night for the next day.

❖ Ensure wake-up calls are cheerful, positive, and laced with love.

❖ Be sure your child eats breakfast when possible, even if they are not hungry. Get them used to putting something in their stomachs every morning. If they will eat breakfast at school instead, schedule to get them there in time so that they can eat without having to rush and gobble the food.

❖ When you say farewell to your children, be sure it is with love and positive wishes for a great day. A hug as they leave to catch the bus or as you leave for work while they wait for the bus or a quick kiss as they exit the car at drop off. Even if you have to give words of correction for something during the morning routine, ensure you leave them with a positive feeling to begin their day's activities. This lays the foundation for you to have a wonderful day.

After School:

❖ Be sure that your children have age-appropriate care after school.

❖ Although many adults believe middle-school-age children can be at home alone after school (called latchkey kids), this is not the recommendation by the professionals.

❖ Middle-school-age children need adult supervision.

❖ Latchkey kids are prone to get into trouble, are more susceptible to misbehavior, and are actually more prone to anxiety when left on their own consistently.

❖ This age group needs to come home to an adult who is a safe haven, a parent, grandparent, adult family friend, or participate in some kind of after school program.

❖ For teens, parents should establish some call in or check-in routines. The fact that they are teens means you need to know where they are and who they are with.

<u>Evenings:</u>

❖ Evening is the time most family members navigate to separate parts of the house, each doing their own thing. This is not the way to build family collaboration and unity.

❖ At the very least, dinner should be a time for family members to bond. As often as possible, all family members should eat together at the dinner table, preferably; but at least watching a family values program on television.

❖ Use family dinner time to share the day's activity, listen to what your children experienced during the day, and connect in communication. Everyone should be encouraged to talk and share. Negative comments and criticism should be discouraged and saved for individual discussion.

❖ Either before dinner or after, homework should be made a priority. Parents should ask about homework assignments.

<u>Bedtime:</u>

❖ On school nights, children need a regular time to go to sleep.

❖ Younger children should have a designated bedtime each night with a regular routine that helps them relax and wind down. Routines might include storytelling, reading aloud, conversation, and songs. Avoid too much excitement though as it must be a wind-down time that leads to rest, relaxation, and sleep

❖ Teens can just be given the latest time when lights should be out. You should also spend some time with them as well. They may not have a 'bedtime,' but you can still usher them to a place of relaxation as they prepare for sleep.

Your routine with them should incorporate a time for them to talk while you listen with the ultimate goal of them wanting to talk to you about their lives, their problems, their concerns, and their plans.

❖ 'Lights out' time can be different for different aged children.

Weekends:

❖ Weekends are good times for family togetherness. You should always plan something for family togetherness. It does not have to be outside the home; does not have to incur extra cost; and does not have to take a lot of time, especially when teens often have their own schedules.

❖ The family activities can be shopping together, visiting a museum, city events or landmarks, going to a park, biking, or simply going to church together.

❖ Keep in mind that as you plan family time, you'll also allow them to have their quiet time and 'friends' time.

Establishing Routine Norms

Child psychologists strongly suggest establishing routines early in a child's life, preferably from birth, to make it easier to make practicing routines an easy family norm. However, if that has not been a norm in your family, you can begin to establish household routines at any time with children of any age, including teens. Just be advised that older children may take more time to get use to the new rules of the household, and may initially give some resistance. Don't let the resistance hinder your establishing routines that will make your life and the lives of your children better.

Step 1: Making the shift from no or minimum routines to a more structured household is a big step in your family dynamic. Don't make the decisions or decide the areas to focus on lightly. Have a family meeting to discuss what needs to change, why it needs to change, the benefits to the child and the family, and what the expectations to make the change are. If your children are younger school-aged, the conversation should be more instructional; if you have older children, especially teens, more discussion is mandatory.

For parents with older children, as you discuss expectations, allow them to give their ideas about implementation strategy. The more you can incorporate their ideas, the easier it will be to get them to buy-in, cooperate, and abide by the expectations. During your initial family meeting to establish family routines, listen to your children and their concerns. Be as open-minded in incorporating their suggestions where you can. Be absolutely sure that establishing a routine is something you are positive you want to do for your family. It is better to avoid the issue, rather than start to establish a routine, then give up on the process.

Step 2: Establish the important times in the family routines. A standard mealtime for family dinners is wonderful, especially if a routine will be family meals together. For younger children, routine bedtimes and nap times are crucial to minimize the push back at bedtime. If you currently have no family schedule, gradually move to a consistent routine. With older children, if there have been no established routines, make the implementation of the new routines a family project. Talk to them about what is desired, why it is deemed important, and allow them to provide input. Wherever possible, use their feedback in executing new routines.

Step 3: Be patient during the shift. The transition for younger children will be easier than for older children, as already mentioned. It will take expressions of love, explanations of whys, and consistency of practice to help children become accustomed to the new family norms and routines. For older children, you will need to exhibit patience until the expected activities and behaviors become family routines. Do not exhibit frustration if the routine does not happen as quickly as you would like. Under no circumstance should you revert to not having a routine. Remember, the goal of establishing routines is to makes your family stronger, more unified, and serve as a tool to help your child be more successful in school and life.

Step 4: Since establishing a routine in your family will be a new family process, if you find the need to adjust the plan at any time, do so. You don't want to stop what you start, but as with any plan, if you find something is not working as you'd hoped and a better way presents itself, make the change. The purpose of a routine is to *help* your family, not hinder progress or make things more difficult. Just remember to communicate with your children so they understand what is going on and why the change is needed.

Homework Monitoring Strategies

How closely you need to monitor your child's homework process depends upon the age of your child, how well-established homework routines are, how independent he or she is, and how well he or she does in school. Whatever the age of your child, if assignments are not getting done satisfactorily, more supervision is needed.

❖ Read everything that is sent home with your child at the beginning of the school year. A lot of information is provided related to various school policies and student expectations. At all ages, you need to review this information carefully.

❖ If it is not included in the information sent home with the student, ask the school about the School's Homework Policy. Read it carefully, and ask about anything that you do not understand.

❖ For elementary-age students, homework should be monitored very closely on a daily basis. It must be very hands-on, providing guidance during homework completion.

❖ For middle-school-age students, monitoring can be less hands-on. It should involve reviewing the homework upon completion and asking when and where they need help.

❖ For high school students, monitoring should include checking in to ensure that homework assignments are taking priority over social interactions and making yourself available to assist when you are needed. Just because they are in high school does not mean they no longer need monitoring; they just need it in a different way. They still need your involvement.

❖ At the start of the school year, ask the teacher the following:
- What kinds of assignments will be given?
- How long are children expected to take to complete them?
- How does the teacher want you to be involved?

- How often will parent-teacher conferences be held?

Lay a Success Foundation

Ask your child's teacher what they need you to do related to homework assignments and what they expect of parents. Do they want you to just check to make sure the assignment is done, or should you do something more? Some teachers want parents to go over the homework and point out errors, while others ask parents to simply check to make sure the assignment is completed. It's also good to ask the teacher to call you if any problems with homework come up. You need to know if the dog that you don't have is eating homework assignments ☺. Help make your child's teacher's job easier by following some simple rules of student engagement.

Be Available

Elementary school students often like to have someone in the same room when working on assignments in case they have questions. For a busy mom, this can be as simple as having a homework corner close to the kitchen so that while mom prepares dinner, she can monitor the homework being completed. If your child is cared for by someone else, talk to that person about what you expect regarding homework. For an older child, if no one will be around, ensure that the expectations of homework completion are very clear.

As a parent, you can show your engagement and reinforce expectations by calling them after school and take just a couple of minutes to ask about the school day and what homework has been assigned. This sends a dual message to your older child. It tells them that you are genuinely interested in their day and their concerns, and that you take their educational journey

36

as seriously as you want them to take it. It will also serve to give you peace of mind that they are where you expect them to be, and they are safe.

Give It the Once-Over

Looking over homework assignments will look differently for the different age students.

❖ Generally, working through homework assignments with your elementary school child should be an easy task.

- Despite busy schedules, make time to work with your child to complete homework assignments, so they learn at an early age, how important the homework process is.

- I explained to my children that just as my primary job outside the home was human resource management; their primary job outside the home was to be successful in school. If either of us failed at our jobs, there would be serious consequences.

- If you are not available to help your young child, look critically at your available source of help. This is essential in helping your child understand the importance of school and education. Just note, that as you assess your resources to help you, choose wisely to ensure that the person or persons that you choose can be trusted with your child.

❖ When homework is reviewed by the teacher and returned, for younger students, read the comments to see if your child has done the assignments satisfactorily. Share the comments, good and not so good, with your child to reinforce the message of expectations.

❖ For your junior high school students, be sure to review the finished assignments.

  ▪ If you're not there when an assignment is finished, look it over when you get home. Remember, the goal is to consistently reinforce your message of expectations and the importance of education.

  ▪ If you get home after they are asleep, ensure that part of your routine is for them to leave the assignment at a place where you can see it and look it over.

❖ For high school students, you don't need to check routine assignments on a daily because you want to begin to instill a sense of responsibility in them. However, you should consistently ask about how assignments are going.

  ▪ Give them the gift of your trust when asking about routine homework assignments until or unless they prove they can't be trusted to follow through.

❖ With your high schoolers, ensure that you are connected in communicating with your teen's teachers to obtain feedback on how things are going, as well as scheduling regular parent-teacher conferences.

  ▪ For major projects, take more interest, and get more involved in reviewing the projects as they work on it, and letting them know you are available to help when they need you.

  ▪ This is how you can begin to promote them to make independent decisions while ensuring they know you are just a nod away when they need help.

  ▪ Have conversations with their teachers to ensure that you are doing all you can to ensure the projects are successful.

❖ Your participation in school activities will let you know if your older child is not doing homework as expected. If your trust is found to be misplaced, then take a stricter approach to monitoring the high schooler's homework completion.

Television and Homework Impact

American children, on average, spend far more time watching television than they do completing homework. Studies support that it is easier to get homework done and get assignments correct when television time is limited. Television viewing has a major impact on the development of children and adolescents. According to research statistics, youth in the United States watch an average of three to four hours of television a day on weekdays and significantly more on weekends. By the time a teen graduate high school, they will have spent more time watching television than they have in the classroom. While television can entertain, inform, and keep our children company, it can also influence them in very undesirable ways.

Time spent watching television takes away from important developmental activities such as:
❖ Reading
❖ Homework and school assignments
❖ Playing and exercise
❖ Family interactions
❖ Social development.

Children also learn information from television that may be inappropriate or incorrect. They often cannot tell the difference between the fantasy presented on television and what is reality. They are easily influenced by the thousands of commercials; reality television shows, which are seldom reality by the way; movies that give very poor lessons of human interactions; and glamorization of celebrities who should never be glamorized.

Younger children are impressionable and may assume that what they see on television is typical, safe, and acceptable. Older children who are prone to emotional reactions may be prone to experiment more than would be normal without the influence of television. As a result, television exposes children to behaviors and attitudes that may be overwhelming with unexpected outcomes.

Children who watch a lot of television unsupervised or unchecked generally exhibit the following:

❖ Lower grades in school
❖ Read fewer books
❖ Exercise less
❖ Prone to overweight

However, involved and active parenting can ensure that television watching does not have to be a negative experience. Parents can counter negative influences by doing the following:

❖ Parents should turn off shows that they feel are inappropriate for the child.

❖ Parents should also have discussions with their children to set the parameters of television watching and ensure the following:

    ▪ Don't allow children to watch long blocks of television but help them select individual programs that are age-appropriate and enjoyable.

- Choose shows that meet the developmental needs of your child. Children's shows on public TV are appropriate, but soap operas, adult sitcoms, and adult talk shows are not.

- Set certain periods when the television will be off. Study times are for learning, not for sitting in front of the TV doing homework. Meal times are a good time for family members to talk with each other, not for watching television.

Watch Television with Your Child

The most impactful thing a parent can do to counter the negative effects of television viewing is to watch TV with your child. Be intentional about what you watch with your child, and consider them when you decide what to watch.

❖ Encourage discussions with your children about what they are seeing as you watch shows with them. Point out positive behavior, such as cooperation, friendship, and concern for others.

❖ While watching television, make connections to history, books, places of interest, and personal events.

❖ Talk about your personal and family values as they relate to the show.

❖ Ask children to compare what they are watching with real events. Talk about the realistic consequences of violence.

❖ Encourage your child to watch shows related to what your child enjoys and is actively involved in, such as hobbies and sports.

With proper guidance, your child can learn to use television healthily and positively.

Balance Homework & Television

Once you and your child have worked out a homework schedule, take time to discuss the schedule with your child, tell them how much television is permissible and what programs they can and cannot watch. Your teen may not be happy when you limit them watching some of the 'popular' programs. However, what is popular does not always send the messages that your child needs to embrace to be successful. Talk to them about your family values and how the show they want to watch does not support those values. This is the key - if you insist on not watching something because of family values, your lifestyle needs to reflect what you say. For instance, you can't tell them that a show is prohibited because of the profanity; but you use profanity when you get upset. Children emulate what they see and experience more than what you say.

It's worth noting that television can be a learning tool. Look for programs that relate to what your child is studying in school, i.e., programs on history or science or dramatizations of children's literature. Also, identify shows that support family unity, community strength, and positive messaging. When you can, watch shows with your child, discuss what has been viewed, and consider follow-up activities that might reinforce what you and your child watched, such as reading up on the subject, a trip to the museum, etc.

Balance Helping & Doing

The basic rule is, "It's not your homework - it's your child's." So, don't get so involved in the assignment that you do the assignment. Doing assignments for your child won't help them

42

understand and use information, and it won't help him become confident in his own abilities. Your job is to help, encourage, and support your child in doing the work that has been assigned.

Give Praise Often

People of all ages respond to praise. Children need that level of encouragement on a continuous basis from the people whose opinions they value most - their parents and primary caregivers. *"This is such a great job for your first try!"* or *"This is so creative; you are so smart!"* These types of encouraging statements go a long way toward motivating your child to complete assignments; and even further towards laying a foundation for them to believe in themselves.

Your child is taking in and personalizing every word you say to them and every action you take towards them. Your words become the foundation of what they believe about themselves. So, even when they have not done their best work, be cautious of how you say what you say. Hold them accountable; but make criticism constructive and something that builds them up rather than tear them down while holding them accountable. Instead of telling your child, *"You aren't going to hand in that mess, are you?"*; try this approach: *"The teacher will understand your ideas better if you use your best handwriting."* Then give praise when the improved work is completed.

Homework Discussions

Talk to your child about their assignments. This will help them think through the instructions and break the assignment down into manageable parts. This is critical for younger students as well as high schoolers. Remember, just because they are older does not mean they don't need you to be actively involved in their day-to-day. They just need you to be involved in a different capacity. Below are some questions you can ask to get the dialogue flowing.

❖ *Do you understand everything you're supposed to do with the assignment?*
After your child has read the instructions, ask him or her to tell you in their own words what the assignment is about. If your child can't read yet or seems to have trouble understanding the assignment, this is a prime opportunity for family connection. For younger ages, you can read the assignment to your child. For older ages, you can read and discuss your interpretation and your child's interpretation to come to a determination of how to proceed.

If there is confusion about an assignment, never just tell the child what you think needs to be done and tell them to do it. Talk to the child to get them thinking in terms of what they learned in school to help determine the assignment's purpose. There will also likely be times when the assignment is confusing to you. Don't freak out or tell them to 'figure it out.' Help them identify the source of the confusion. Are there words they don't understand? Do they understand what is being asked? If neither you nor your child understands an assignment, call a classmate or contact the teacher. Your involvement at the beginning of the assignment can be the key to your child completing the assignment successfully. Some schools have homework hotlines you can call for assignments in case your child misplaced a paper or was absent that day. Be sure to get this information from your child's teacher at the beginning of the school.

❖ *Do you need help in understanding what to do?*
Discuss with your child if they have the knowledge and information they need to complete the assignment. Talk to them to assess if any additional instruction is needed to complete the homework successfully. For example, for a math assignment, do they have the knowledge they need to solve the math problems; if a history assignment, do they need to read resources outside of the assigned textbook? If any areas need additional attention, help your child where it's needed; or call the school to get some additional assistance from the teacher. You must be your child's best resource and advocate for them to be successful.

❖ *Do you have everything needed for the assignment?*
Be sure your child has what is needed to complete the assignment. Sometimes he or she may need special supplies, such as colored pencils, metric rulers, maps, or reference books. As mentioned before, check with the teacher, school guidance counselor, or principal for possible sources of assistance if you have budgetary constraints and don't have funds to purchase special supply needs. Your local resource is an invaluable resource for published resource needs.

❖ *Does your answer make sense to you?*
Once the assignment has been completed, ask your child to review the homework and let you know if it makes sense to them. Sometimes the answer to a math problem may not seem logical, or the meaning of a paragraph your child has written is unclear. If it is not clear to you or if they do not clearly understand what they have completed, that is a clue that they may not have a strong foundation of understanding. If that is the case, they will likely not be able to be successful in learning the next level of study.

Be sure your child is strong in their understanding of each level of learning, so they do not fall behind. Always remember that your child's teacher is there to help you help your child succeed.

Homework can bring together children, parents, and teachers in a common effort to improve student learning. However, it is critically important that parents do their part in the educational process. Parents and teachers must work together to ensure a child's success in the classroom. The younger your child is when you start to do the kinds of activities suggested in this guide, the better. However, any age is a good age to start because a child, at any age, needs a parent's time, support, and validation to be successful.

Helping your child with homework is an opportunity to improve your child's chances of doing well in school and life. By helping your child with homework, you can help them learn important lessons about discipline and responsibility, which are lessons that will lay the foundation for success throughout their lives. You are the key to ensuring open lines of communication between you and your child, and you and the school. You are also in a unique position to help your child make connections between schoolwork and the "real world," and thereby bring meaning (and some fun) to your child's homework experience.

CHAPTER 4
SUCCESS-BASED HOME CULTURE

"At the end of the day, the most overwhelming key to a child's success is the positive involvement of parents." Jane Hull

Creating a success culture in the home begins with ensuring you have routines and strategies at home that fully support what the child is learning from his or her teachers in school. That means, as a parent, you must set parameters in your home that support homework is the most important task your child must complete when they get home from school. Each kind of homework has a critical role in positioning your child for a successful educational journey as well as being a success in life.

Reading Homework Tips

Statistics support the following dismal statistics related to the reading capacity of U.S. citizens:

❖ There are more than 32 million U.S. citizens who can't read.

❖ 19% of high school graduates are leaving high school with minimum to no reading skills.

❖ Graduates who have no or low reading skills will live at or below the poverty level as they will not have the fundamental skill needed to function in today's society.

❖ Graduates who have no or low reading skills generally live life with minimum joy since day-to-day activities that many people take for granted become a source of frustration, anger, and fear for those who cannot read proficiently.

❖ Poor readers often have poor self-image or low self-esteem due to feelings of inadequacy.

❖ Students with no or low reading skills cannot perform other subjects successful because they cannot read and understand the material associated with the class.

The capacity to read well is one of the strongest skills a child needs to master at an early age in order to be positioned to master all other educational endeavors. This is the skill that is fundamental to developing the mind and laying a foundation for a child to be successful in all other areas of learning. Teaching children to read at a young age helps develop language skills, master listening skills, and increase proficiency in the overall ability to communicate well. The earlier a child begins to master reading skills, the more they improve the capacity to expand their vocabulary and further enhances success in school and life.

Following are strategies parents can employ to encourage reading proficiency and make reading fun for the child.

Your Elementary Aged Child:

❖ Have your child read aloud to you every night. If you start this early (before they start school or in elementary school), ready will become something that your child enjoys throughout life.

❖ Choose a quiet place, free from distractions, for your child to do his nightly reading assignments. Don't leave them alone for the whole time. Spend time with them while they read.

❖ As your child reads, point out spelling and sound patterns such as cat, pat, hat, etc. Make it fun; make it a game.

❖ When your child reads aloud to you and makes a mistake, point out the words that are missed and help them read the word correctly. Don't chastise or rebuke; this will only make them not want to read.

❖ After your child has stopped to correct a word they read, have them go back and reread the entire sentence from the beginning to make sure they understand what the sentence is saying.

❖ When the reading assignment is done, ask your child to tell you in their own words what happened in a story.

❖ To check your child's understanding of what they are reading, occasionally pause and ask questions about the characters and events in the story.

❖ Ask your child why they think a character acted in a certain way; have them to support their answer with information from the story.

❖ Before getting to the end of a story, ask your child what they think will happen next and why.

Your Middle-School-Aged Child:

❖ For middle-school-age children, don't assume that just because they are getting older, they don't need or are not interested in the hands-on approach to helping them with reading.

❖ For school assignments, begin to loosen the reigns a little and allow them to read independently, then come to summarize what they read to you.

▪ This means you may also need to read whatever is assigned to be prepared for their summary to you.

❖ To encourage them towards the enjoyment of reading, take

them to the library or bookstore.

- Allow them to check out or purchase the book of their choice, even if it's not quite your cup of tea.

- Middle-school-aged youth are entering a stage of development whereby they are learning to be their authentic selves, and want to feel a little grown-up. An excellent way to help at this stage is to begin to respect that place. Ask them critical questions about the book they are reading. Allow them to debate with you, respectfully, of course. Help them think critically about what they read.

❖ Pay attention to what your child is interested in, i.e., favorite movie, hobby, what excites them in conversation. Whatever it is, connect it to a reading source; find something printed related to the area of interest at their reading level to capture their reading attention.

❖ Model what you want to see in your child. Adolescents will more likely engage in what they see you do, rather than just what you say. If you want to see them reading more, let them see your enjoyment of reading.

❖ If your child is struggling with reading, don't be critical. Keep things as positive as possible by meeting your child where he or she is. Encourage them to take baby steps and be sure not to be condemning or intimidating in your responses. Praise their progress, no matter how small.

❖ Reading a series in its order of publication is always exciting for a child. If you find a topic that interests them, and there is any series out there, be sure to start with the first book. It will build the excitement for the next book, and you won't have to work too hard to get them to check out or purchase the next reading challenge.

Your High-School-Aged Child:

❖ If your teenager is having struggles reading by the time they are in high school, you will need to take a targeted interest to help them catch up. If they don't catch up, they will struggle for the rest of their lives.

❖ Struggling teens read slowly because they have to spend so much time on the process called decoding. Decoding is how the mind translates printed words into sounds by breaking down each syllable to sound out the word.

❖ Teens who have difficulty reading spend a lot of time on the decoding process, which causes several issues:

- In spending excessive time trying to decode and sound out the words, the meaning of the sentence gets lost.

- If the meaning is lost, they will get frustrated and anxious about the entire reading process.

- When reading is difficult, they won't be able to master any of the other classes, which leads to embarrassment and frustration with the overall educational process, which means poor performance and low grades.

❖ For teens who are experiencing this level of difficulty, as a parent, you need to talk to your child's school about how to best engage a reading specialist to help your child.

- NOTE: This needs to be done as confidentially as possible to minimize embarrassment to your teen. Embarrassing a teen is one of the #1 no-no's of their existence. Honor your teen by helping him, or her maximize their potential without putting them in a position where they may feel embarrassed or ridiculed for what they don't know.

❖ Encourage your teen in their interests and areas you notice they are gifted. EVERY child has some areas that come naturally to them. They don't often understand what makes them special. That's where you come in.

- Whatever their something is, find a book or articles about that area, and present it to them. Encourage them to read what you found, review the information with them, and praise them for how good they are at it.

- You will be amazed at how your interest and encouragement will inspire your child to learn more through reading.

- Every time they come to you with what they find in reading, no matter what you have going on, take time to talk to them and discuss the information.

❖ The best way to encourage your teen to read is to let them see you reading about things that interest them. Talk to them about what you read. Ask their opinions and allow them to speak openly to you about what they think.

- Through this process, you will provide some great lessons for your teen, to include letting them know that you feel their interests matter, that they have a voice and they need to use it, and their opinions are important and have value.

If you are not a good reader yourself, the process of helping your child embrace reading is an excellent opportunity for you to master this skill as well. Both you and your child can read, learn, and grow together. Too many parents are embarrassed when they don't have the skill to assist their child in a school assignment. However, by admitting your short-coming and engaging your child to learn a new skill, you are teaching your child one of the greatest lessons in life — that they do not have to settle for where you are right now. They should be determined to do whatever it takes to improve themselves and pursue their goals.

Math Homework Tips

Math has to be the one area that EVERY parent has heard their child say, 'why do I need to learn math?' With the advent of technology like cell phones and quick access to bank account information, many young people just don't understand why math is so important. Sometimes, while seeking to help children with homework, parents may have the same question. But rest assured, learning math is so much more than just adding and subtracting numbers.

Several research studies suggest that a child's capacity to become proficient in math early on the educational journey is a foundational predictor of future academic success.

❖ The earlier math skills are learned and mastered, the more likely the strong aptitude in high school math and greater potential for going to college.

❖ A 2014 study actually suggested that early competency in math skills was a predictor of a person's creative contributions and leadership proficiency in adulthood.

❖ In addition to basic mathematical equation learning (adding, subtracting, multiplication, and division), math teaches logic and order, which are critical life skills in day to day success.

❖ Some companies in the U.S. prefer to hire math majors for other areas of specialty related to strategy because there is the presumption that these graduates will have more critical thinking skills.

❖ Through math, children learn the general principles of calculating percentages and fractions. People use these skills in simple daily activities such as preparing a recipe, deciding to take a car trip, evaluating if a clearance item is a good deal, making a major purchase, or preparing and managing a budget.

❖ Students who master math skills, generally seek higher degree pursuits and tend to land higher-paying jobs.

❖ Students with strong math skills consistently score higher on assessment exams (SATs and ACTs) and, thus, obtain more scholarships and higher secondary educational opportunities.

Educational research supports that one of the major components of a child's desire to learn and master math is the parent's attitude about math. If parents are positive, children engage in learning math. If parents are negative, children tend to have a harder time learning math skills. As a parent, you must encourage your child to excel in this area, as this will enhance life-long opportunities for success. Below are strategies to help your child embrace math and be excited about the math learning journey. These strategies apply to children of all ages. Parents just need to determine to what degree to apply the strategy to their child, depending on the child and their learning style.

❖ Encourage your child to use a daily math assignment book to keep track of what is required and due dates.

❖ Follow the progress your child is making in math. Check with your child daily about his homework.

❖ If you don't understand your child's math assignments, engage in frequent communication with his or her teacher.

Do not feel embarrassed to tell the teacher that you don't understand an assignment. It's all about providing a strong learning foundation for your child.

❖ If your child is experiencing problems in math, contact the teacher to learn whether he or she is working at grade level and what can be done at home to help improve academic progress. Ask your child's teacher if they think the problem could be math anxiety. If so, find out what you can do to help them overcome the anxiety and be successful in the class.

❖ Request that your child's teacher schedule after-school math tutoring sessions if your child really needs help. Sometimes you must insist that the school provides any support needed to help your child succeed. Even in insisting, do so with collaboration and respect to ensure you maintain a positive relationship for your child.

❖ If feasible, advocate for the use of research-based peer tutoring programs for math in your child's school. These tutoring programs have proven results, and students truly enjoy them.

❖ Use household chores as opportunities for reinforcing math learning such as cooking and repair activities, or any other activity that requires measuring or numbers.

❖ Be mindful and aware of how your child is being taught math, and don't teach strategies and shortcuts that conflict with the approach the teacher is using.

❖ Check in with the teacher and ask what you can do to help your child master what is being taught. Help them see math as something fun instead of being something to fear.

❖ Ask the teacher about online resources that you can use with your child at home.

❖ At the beginning of the year, ask your child's teacher for a list of suggestions that will enable you to help your child with math homework.

Science Homework Tips

Although science is not one of the 3 R's – Reading, wRiting, and Rithmetic – it is one of the critical areas of the educational journey. Science is just as critical to the learning and educational process as mathematics because of the mass impact on a child's critical thinking and problem-solving skills. The younger a child begins to embrace knowledge of science, the stronger a child's capacity to employ strong logic skills, problem-solving skills, perseverance.

Science taps into a child's natural curiosity and can be seen everywhere in everyday living. Everything we experience related to today's technology is science-driven. The simple act of getting in a car and driving the car from one point to another is science-driven. The roadways, traffic lights, and city or town infrastructure are all benchmarked in understanding science. When a child looks outside his or her window or goes outside to play, the impact of science is all around them from the sunlight to the trees and grasses, to the air we breathe.

Science teaches children about how our earth and world functions, the critical importance of our natural resources, and the impact of various weather conditions. Children need to embrace science and the vast possibilities of learning and mastering science skills. Below are strategies you can use as a parent to help your child of any age to master the science educational journey.

❖ Encourage your child to talk about the science that they learned in class.

❖ Talk about how you use science at home and work.

❖ Look for activities that require your child to use their science skills. For example, a walk in your backyard is filled with science (i.e., ecology, evolution, biology).

❖ When your child gets stuck, encourage your children to figure out as much as they can by themselves.

❖ Watch science-related programs on the Discovery Channel and the Science Channel then discuss the concepts in the program.

❖ With specific assignments, encourage them to review the work that was done in class. The homework is always the practice of the skills that were presented in class.

❖ Encourage the student to focus first on what they know. What information do they already have? What are you trying to find out?

Test Taking Terrors

Talk frankly to your child about test-taking, to include if they get test anxiety. Let them know it is not abnormal, but they can manage it. Test anxiety is defined as *a feeling of tense distress associated with test-taking, which impacts a student's ability to retain studied information and successfully perform on the test.* Some test anxiety is natural and will generally prompt a student to get mentally focused and physically alert in approaching test-taking. However, too much anxiety can result in physical anguish, emotional upset, and concentration difficulties. When this occurs as a natural response to test-taking, it will negatively impact the student's capacity to be successful in school; and can impact confidence in every other area of life.

Test Taking Reactions

❖ Physiological reactions to test anxiety include rapid heartbeat, muscle tension, queasiness, dry mouth, or perspiration.

❖ Psychological reactions include feelings of nervousness, fear, worry, distress, and self-doubt.

❖ Behavioral reactions include an inability to act, make decisions, express oneself, or to deal with everyday situations.

❖ If your child has test anxiety, telling them to 'get over it' is one of the worse things you can do. This makes them feel that you don't understand and don't care about their feelings or what they are going through.

❖ In order to help them, you will need to help them get in a calm and confident place as they go into the test-taking environment.

Managing Test Anxiety

Below are some of the best tips to address test anxiety and best strategies for preparing for test-taking in general.

❖ **Have a Positive Attitude**

Approach the test experience as an adventure. Success takes planning, time, and commitment. The same focus should be taken as a student thinks about an upcoming test. It might seem like it's going to be a difficult task, but the right mindset can make the journey much easier.

❖ **Plan to Succeed**

The week before the test, students should ask their teacher what the test is going to cover. Is it from the textbook only, class notes, or a combination? For math, can you use your calculator?

- If they have missed any classes due to absences, they should be sure to get the notes from the teacher or from classmates who have proven to be good students.
- Students should ensure that they don't want to take notes from students who don't perform.
- They should make a list of the most important discussion points covered and use that as a guide when they study; circle challenging topics and discussion points that will require extra study time.
- Plan to spend the extra time to become comfortable with those areas.

❖ AVOID Cramming…It's Surefire Failure

Trying to cram the night before a test doesn't work. This is especially true for students who have test-taking anxiety. Cramming is a set up for failure.

- Encourage your child to follow a well laid out study plan. The only thing that should happen the night before is a quick material review and an early bedtime.
- The brain and body needs sleep to function well. Staying up late will undermine a strong study regimen.
- The brain needs rest in order to function well. The less rest your child gets before a test, the stronger the possibility that they won't do as well on the test as they could.

❖ The Morning of the Test

DO NOT go without breakfast! The brain functions better when a child has had adequate nourishment; so, make sure your child has a nutritious breakfast.

- **Avoid high sugar breakfast foods.** The temporary boost of energy from the sugar will eventually lead to them crashing.

- After a good breakfast, ensure that your child gets to school early so that they can do a ten-minute power study right before the test. Not a cram, but a quick review, which helps the brain become alert and ready for taking a test.

- Ensure that your child has everything they need for the test before they leave home - scratch paper, extra pencils, a calculator (if allowed).

❖ **Test Time**

Ensure you discuss with your child to let them know you have confidence that they can be successful. Just the voice of your assurance will give them confidence and courage. Review test-taking strategies with them the night before or the morning of the test. This should be your strategy with children of all ages, including your teenagers. Don't assume just because they've taken tests before they should have it down pat. News flash, they generally don't ☺ . So, take time to review these basic with them for test taking success:

- Before the test, take a few deep breaths to relax.

- Avoid any conversations or situations that could lead to being upset or irritated.

- Have a clear understanding of how the test will be scored and what constitutes passing.

- Briefly review the test to assess what areas may require more time and attention.

- Read the instructions carefully to ensure a clear understanding of what is being asked. Then answer questions they are certain they know first - ones that can be completed quickly to promote confidence.

- Once they have answered the questions they know, come back to those that require more work or for which they are unsure of the answer.

Test Taking Hindrances

Be sure to discuss aspects of test-taking that can disrupt a well-planned test-taking strategy. The more you talk to them about what may happen, the less they will be thrown off course if it or when it actually happens.

❖ **"I'm Stuck...What do I do?!"**

One question that a student does not know or does not understand can knock a student off balance for the remainder of the test.

- They mustn't get worried or frustrated. It will make the situation worse.

- They should reread the question to make sure they understand it; then give it their best to resolve it.

- If still stuck, they should circle it and move on. They can come back to it later if time permits.

- If they have no idea about the answer, they should make a best guess unless leaving it blank won't be held against them. That only applies to certain types of tests.

❖ **Multiple-Choice Questions**

Generally, in a multiple-choice question, you can eliminate a couple of responses immediately.

- The process of elimination can help the student to narrow down to the potential best choices.

- The student should choose from those options based on what they know about the subject matter.

❖ **Neatness Counts**

If a student's 4s look like 9s, it could be a problem.

- The student must be sure that writing is legible and understandable.

- They must also be sure to erase mistakes completely, which is one reason a student should never take a test in ink unless directed to do so by the teacher.

- For machine-scored tests, spaces must be filled in carefully.

❖ **"I'm Done!"**

Not so fast - when the last item is complete on the test, impress on your student that if there is time left to use the time wisely.

- When students have answered the last question, if time is left, go back to review their answers, making sure that they didn't make any careless mistakes (such as putting the right answer in the wrong place or skipping a question).

- They should spend the last remaining minutes going over the hardest problems before turning in the test.

Dealing with Specific Students Traits

Understanding your child is the most critical thing you must learn as a parent. According to child psychologist, Robert Myers, to effectively guide and nurture your child as they grow into who they are meant to be, you must be able to recognize when things are not going well in your child's world. You need to know when to draw closer to them to help them cope; and when to give them room to wobble as they learn to deal with some situations on their own.

To get to a level of understanding your child, you must be consistently mindful that although child development support that children will have things in common that all children go through, our child is a unique person with a unique personality. As with every person, they will have strong character traits as well as some traits that may not be as positive. Trying to make your child be someone he or she is not will only result in a child who lacks confidence, may draw into a shell, or may become rebellious. Either way, the result will be a child who is hindered from reaching their full potential.

Your job as a parent is to let your child know by *your actions and behaviors* towards them that they are wonderful creations, capable of great things. Don't ever doubt that your opinion matters. What you think, say, and project about your child is the foundation of what they believe of themselves. Your primary job as a parent is not to just provide shelter, clothing, and food; but to know who your child is, and in the process to help mold them into who they are going to be. By God's design, they have greatness within. However, they need you to help cultivate and pull it out of them.

You must be able to recognize if and when your child is going through something that needs your attention. You must be consistently mindful of changes in attitude, behaviors, eating habits, sleep habits, play habits, etc. When you realize some issues may hinder their greatness, you will need to work with them to address the issues to ensure they are still positioned for success. Below are some of the most common imperfections a child may have that you, as a parent, need to help them deal with to chart a path for success.

The Disorganized Student

Contrary to popular belief, these students are not lazy or purposely disobedient. Their poor performance is not a matter of needing to try harder. It's not that simple. These students have as much potential to succeed in school as any other student; they just need more support than the average student to find that success.

❖ Plan a time to have a talk with your student about helping them. The key is not to start this conversation with an insult about how disorganized or messy things are.

❖ Give them words of encouragement about their potential and acknowledge their efforts in what they do.

❖ Help them organize their book bags and their study area.

❖ Prepare a set time each week to sit with them to discuss their organization strategy to help keep them on task.

The Forgetful Student

According to psychologists Stephen and Marianne Garber, children are especially prone to the Forgetful Syndrome, whereby forgetting and misplacing things is a natural occurrence. It can be frustrating, time-consuming, and maddening for parents. Some are more prone to being forgetful than others. However, getting upset with and penalizing the child will not make things better. In fact, that reaction promotes a lack of self-confidence and lessens the capacity to succeed.

Many parents tend to think when a child reaches the 'age of reasoning,' approximately seven years of age, that they should be responsible little people and magically able to reason, organize, and plan things out. This is so far from the reality of what their little minds can conceive. Young children still need guidance from parents to develop strategies that will help them remember what they need. This is one of the biggest and best strategies you can impress upon them that will become a lifelong success strategy.

❖ Start by realizing that a child's capacity to reason and remember is not equal to that of an adult. They will not remember 'important' details of things the way you do nor reason out what needs to be done when. If that were the case, they would not need parents or some parental guidance until their early twenties.

❖ Purchase a Remember Kit. This includes items on which they can write things out to reinforce the importance of events:

  ▪ A calendar with big boxes for each day, posted in an imminent place in the home where all can see, and that will be a consistent reminder of activities and events. You can even make this the family important events calendar, which will emphasize that school assignments are important to everyone in the family.

  ▪ Get a packet of markers with assorted colors. Designate different colors for different kinds of family events or different levels of importance.

❖ Have your children write their activities on the calendar? They should write it, not you. Having them write it on the calendar helps to reinforce the memory. It can be further reinforced by letting them choose the marker colors for their school events and activities.

❖ At the start of each week and each day, get with your child to check the calendar until checking it become a habit. Remind your child to check the calendar just as you would remind them to brush their teeth until it becomes part of their weekly or daily school preparation routine. Child psychologists support that routines are how children establish patterns of what is normal as well as set the tone of family expectations.

❖ Get everything needed for the next day laid out the night before to cut down on morning chaos. Once a child, young or older, establish their normal patterns, i.e., their routine, they don't like those norms or routines disrupted. It creates confusion in their mental processing. Decide on a special place to store all that is needed in a place close to the morning exit for easy retrieval.

❖ For school activities, create a *Call List*, a list of three or four classmates they can call on when they forget an assignment. This strategy is mandatory for elementary and middle- school-ages; but should also be encouraged for forgetful high school students. This list is not only a great idea for collaboration on school assignments, but also a valuable tool if something unexpected happens in your child's life, and you need to contact school mates or friends for information. As a parent, you need to know who is influencing your child. This list is a great start for that awareness.

❖ Identify one of the classmates on the Call List to be a primary *Study Buddy*. You should help the younger children determine who this will be. Authorize your older children to identify this person. You should ensure that you introduce yourself to the parents of your child's Study Buddy, since you can expect study buddies to be in constant communication, and may even become friends. At the very least, they will influence each other; and you want to ensure that influence is positive.

The Overwhelmed Student

To be overwhelmed is to feel defeat or devastating distress as a result of something causing excessive anxiety or being too much to handle. One of the clear signals of being overwhelmed or stressed is forgetfulness. We tend to forget basic things when our minds are preoccupied with information, anxiety, or high expectations. This is a difficult situation for adults; it is especially difficult for children.

Signs of being overwhelmed in students include:

❖ Constantly feeling behind on schoolwork.

❖ Worried about how others perceive them.

❖ Feeling like they are letting people down.

❖ Not able to get a handle on various commitments.

❖ Feeling paralyzed in an effort to multitask to get everything done.

❖ Consistently disorganized and frustrated.

❖ Not as reliable as they used to be.

❖ Feeling burn out.

❖ Tense to the point of anger and other intense emotions.

❖ Feeling scattered and unfocused.

If you believe your child is overwhelmed, try the following:

❖ Simplify activities. Help your child sort out priorities and separate the 'have to dos' from 'want to dos.' They generally won't know the difference, or choose those 'to dos' that they **want** to do over what they **must** do.

❖ Clarify what's important. Help them to define what takes priority and what can wait.

❖ Help them create a *Things-To-Do List* on a daily basis. Show them how to list all the actions they must perform, then list them in order of importance.

❖ Have your child take frequent small breaks so as not to stress them out.

Think carefully about how you address certain issues and be careful of the words you use. As a parent, your words have great power. Most child development specialist will tell you that your words shape who your child is and who they have the potential to become. No matter how stubborn or resistant they may appear to be in accepting your guidance; no matter how much they argue with you; no matter how many hurtful things they may say to you in times of anger…know that every word you say to them is being taken in, processed, and accepted as their truth.

Proverbs 18:21 says that the power of life and death lies in the tongue. These words are even more emphatic when those words come from a parent to a child. Make sure your words speak life to your child's spirit and ushers them to a position of success, not failure.

CHAPTER 5
PROMOTE INDEPENDENCE & GROWTH

*"There are two lasting bequests we can give our children.
One is roots. The other is wings."* Hodding Carter, Jr.

One of the hardest things for a loving parent to do is to allow children to work through problems alone and learn from their mistakes. Our driving thought is to keep them from doing something unwise, stepping in the wrong direction, stumbling into the pitfall, and potentially falling hard. It's also hard to know where to draw the line between supporting them through a process and actually doing things for them. If parents continually do things for their children to keep them from difficulty, they will have a difficult time growing into independent, productive people. This critical process starts with their educational journey.

Different teachers have different ideas about the best way for parents to provide guidance to children concerning homework strategies to promote independent thinking. It is critically important that these different expectations do not become a barrier to the child's capacity to learn and engage in the learning process while growing into the independent adults they will become.

A Supportive Learning Posture

Here are a few suggestions with which most teachers agree will continually position you to be supportive of your child while instilling in them a sense of responsibility and accountability in their growth.

❖ Figure Out How Your Child Learns Best

If you understand the style of learning that suits your child, it will be easier for you to help him or her. If you've never thought about your child's learning style before, observe your child.

- Do they seem to work better alone or with someone else?

- If your child gets more done when working with someone else, you may want to consider identifying a classmate to complete assignments with or having them work with a sibling.

- Keep in mind that some homework is meant to be done alone. Check with the teacher before devising a final strategy.

❖ Consider Behavioral Learning Style

Does your child learn better by reading, listening, or doing? Do they learn things best when they can see them?

- If they learn better by seeing, drawing a picture or a chart may help solidify the learning material. For example, after reading a science book, a student may not remember the difference between the tibia and the fibula. However, by drawing a picture of the leg and labeling the bones, they may be able to remember the information easily.

- If they learn better by hearing, it is helpful to read out loud or listen to a recording of the information.

- If they learn by doing, it may be helpful to have them act out what was read or do an exercise related to the learning material.

❖ Help Your Child Get Organized

One of the key strategies to help your child succeed is to set a regular time for children to do homework.

- Put up a calendar on which assignments are posted in a place where you and your child can see it.

- If your child's not able to write yet, then do it for him or her until they can do so for themselves.

- Writing out assignments will get your child used to the idea of keeping track of what's due and when.

- You can also use an assignment book rather than a calendar. It will not have the visual impact of a calendar, but if you can't do a calendar, it's a good secondary plan.

- Homework folders in which students can tuck assignments for safekeeping is also a good organization tool.

❖ Encourage Good Time Management Habits

Teachers give students tips on how to study and will also provide guidance on completing more detailed assignments. You should reinforce these habits and strategies at home, which means there should be a constant dialogue between you and your child's teacher.

- When your child has a detailed project to complete, help them structure a timeline to complete the assignment timely and successfully. For example, if your junior high school student has a science report due in a month, sit down with your child to discuss the project with a potential outline of what's needed.

- For example, a project plan might include the following:

71

- Select a topic
- Determine the focus (what to include)
- Draft an outline
- Conduct the research
- Organize notes
- Write a rough draft
- Make revisions as needed
- Complete the report

- Encourage your child to write down how much time they expect to spend on each step.
  - Dependent upon the age group, help them figure out what they can do on their own and what they need you to assist with.
  - The younger the age, the more you will need to do.
  - Always remember not to do everything for them, whatever the age.
- To identify research sources, encourage your child to expand the search outside of just the Internet.
  - Although this is the Internet age, encourage your child to actually go to the library.
  - Walking through the library aisles and seeing rows of books will provide ideas that can't be experienced just by searching the Internet.
  - The librarian can also be a great resource to provide suggestions on how and where to begin.
  - Many public libraries have homework centers where there are tutors or other kinds of one-on-one assistance.
- After your child has done the research, listen while they explain what they found and how they will develop the project.

- This will help them with communicating their ideas as well as understand how to develop a strategy when it comes to planning a project or detailed homework assignment.
- These are skills that are not only critical in school but also in life.

The Teen Paradigm

Years ago, parents operated under the assumption that once a child hit the adolescent years, the brain was fully developed and functional. As a result, parents put a lot of expectations on teens and were very frustrated when the teen did not react, respond, or otherwise behave as expected. This was especially true when a teen experienced forgetfulness, confusion, and strong emotional reactions.

In recent years, scientists have made a very interesting and eye-opening discovery of which parents must be cognizant. They discovered that *the brain grows just as much during adolescence as it did during early childhood.* That means that just because a child hits 13, the brain does not immediately convert to a posture of logic and wisdom. Rather than become less forgetful, a child is prone to be more forgetful in teen years.

The brain of an adolescent is expanding so rapidly during this growth stage that it does not and cannot operate as efficiently as the adult brain does, or at least as an adult brain should ☺ . In essence, contrary to popular parental beliefs and expectations, your child needs as much or more of you and your time when they are teens than your child does when they are younger. Between adolescent brain development and hormone activity, this is a challenging time of physical and emotional growth for teenagers. They need parents to help them maneuver on the path of growth to adulthood. When as a parent you become less engaging, you are leaving them to fend for themselves when they critically need your guidance.

The reason that your teen can seem disorganized and scattered is that their thought processes are not organized. As the teen years progress, your teen will become more organized and efficient in their thought processes. However, the brain is not fully developed until an individual reaches their mid-20s. Your role during this time of development is to be patient and understand that your teen is not being intentionally defiant or irresponsible. Rather than your anger, they need your tolerance and your support. You can best support your child during this stage by gently, but firmly helping them be better organized and accountable.

Teen Brain Development

❖ Beginning around age 12, you will begin to notice your child exhibits more confusion and forgetfulness, not less. They will need to be reminded about simple tasks, sometimes more than once. Ranting and raving won't help. In fact, responding with anger and frustration will make things worse, as it will negatively impact your relationship. Rather than becoming angry with them, ask them, *"how can I better help you plan and remember what needs to be done?"* They need your guidance, not your criticism.

❖ Although they need you to help them develop habits to enhance memory and accountability, they don't need you to coddle them, which can lead to irresponsibility. Rather, focus on helping them understand they still need to develop a sense of accountability; and help them develop habits and routines to enhance that skill. For example, if they often forget their backpack, lunch, or gym clothes, advise them to keep a checklist posted by the front door, so they see it before they walk out the door. Make them responsible for checking the checklist.

❖ The most powerful part of the teen brain is called the Amygdala (ah-mig-dolla). It is the part of the brain that is driven by emotions and, most critically, the part through which teens interpret situations. This is the reason that teens can often be seen as overly sensitive and taking things too personally. This part of the brain is more active in teen years; it is much stronger than the logic center of the brain. So, expect emotionalism to be a standard part of their responses in various situations.

❖ Although you don't want to hear this, your child will be emotionally driven during most of their teen years. That means, hopefully, you have grown out of your emotionalism and have a high level of emotional intelligence to keep you centered and controlled in your responses and behaviors.

▪ Emotional intelligence is defined as the ability to monitor your emotions, understand your emotional triggers, and control your emotional responses. Simultaneously, you have the ability to assess the emotional temperature of others as it pertains to their actions and reactions to emotional situations.

▪ A parent with low emotional intelligence responds with emotional outbursts when they are met with emotional situations from others, such as responding to anger with anger, and frustration with frustration. This generally leads to loud, hurtful arguments; things said that can't be taken back; and broken relationships.

- A parent with high emotional intelligence is consciously aware of their responses when their child is upset. They can stay calm themselves as they seek to understand the causes of the child's emotional reactions, responses, and outward emotional expressions. They are able to help their teen understand the consequences of their actions, reactions, and negative responses. As a parent, this takes practice, patience, and consistency in applying this concept to interactions with your child. This is critical in helping your teen become more accountable in their actions as they grow and mature.

❖ In the family where the parent or guardian has not outgrown being more emotional than logical (low emotional intelligence), the result is major arguments and communication disconnects between parent and child.

- It is important that if this is the case with you that you work on being stronger in how you respond in emotionally charged situations. Improving one's emotional intelligence mandates self-reflection to understand your emotional triggers and are intentional on controlling emotional responses.

- If your emotional responses are highly charged or volatile, you should consider speaking with someone who can help the healing process from emotional wounds, such as a clinical counselor. If, as a parent, you are just as emotionally charged as your teenager, your household will be more volatile than is healthy for you, your teen, or your household.

❖ Yelling or screaming at your teen because they are emotionally reactive will not work. Since they are emotionally driven, if you respond with low emotional intelligence, this will activate a "fight or flight" response in your teen.

- They will either yell and scream back, which will damage the relationship on both sides, or they will completely shut down. The last thing a parent needs is for a teen to shut down.

- Once a teen shuts down, they may never open back up to you for fear of being judged or of another yelling match. This is the one true paradigm that destroys the foundation of a strong parent-child relationship with teens. But do understand this… if they are not talking to you, they will be talking to someone. Teens have to have an outlet. If your teen shuts down with you and you don't know who they are connecting to, you won't know what kind of influences might be leading them in the wrong direction.

It is also possible that the outlet may be something that is dangerous or unhealthy, such as drugs, alcohol, internet contacts, etc. It is therefore critical that your reactions to your teen's behaviors be more logical, focused, loving, and less emotional so you can provide what your teen needs to grow into the healthy, successfully person they are meant to be.

❖ Increased testosterone in male teens causes negative and aggressive thoughts. Increased estrogen in females causes moodiness. Keep these factors in mind when dealing with your teen.

❖ Alcohol and drugs have a profound negative effect on a teen's already disorganized brain. You will want to be very cognizant of this negative influence related to your child's development.

77

Remember that your teen is experiencing significant changes in brain development during this stage of life. This is the developmental stage when hormones are raging, they are prone to test boundaries, and they are trying to maneuver through the territory of who they will become as adults. How you respond to his or her emotional reactions, forgetfulness, or other actions that you don't want to see will directly impact how they feel about themselves and their vast potential. It will set the stage on how they learn to behave and respond to emotional situations as teens and into adulthood.

De-Compress Emotional Situations

Decompressing is the process of bringing down the emotional charges in cases of negative emotional outbursts. Anger is a natural part of emotional responses and from a developmental perspective, is considered a normal and healthy response to negative outside stressors when things don't go as desired or expected. It is normal to be angry or upset when we are disappointed in how things turned out or when negative things happen that are detrimental to us or those we care about. However, responding in ways that damage others and damage relationships is not healthy and is counter-productive to getting to a helpful outcome.

Various reactions can trigger anger. It can be a result of feeling that something unjust or unfair, feeling criticized or attacked in some way, not getting what was expected or desired, or seeing something that is at odds with what you feel is right. These are just a few reasons that anger can arise and manifest into mild to extreme irritation, varying levels of frustration, exasperation, or extreme angry outbursts. Whatever the cause or the resultant behavior, as a parent, it is crucial that anger is managed with a level of high emotional intelligence that assures you remain in a position to keep the situation from getting out of hand.

Your goals must be to manage the situation between you and your teen in such a way that you do not have regrets about what was said or done, and that the relationship is not destroyed. I made many mistakes with my two eldest when they were teens that resulted in very negative outcomes that prevailed well into their adult years. My responses were based on how I felt rather than what I wanted to accomplish, especially with my eldest child. I responded based on my anger at her instead of reacting to the situation with love and critical thinking. The results were in no way good. Fortunately, by the time my youngest son came along, I had learned some hard lessons and knew how to respond with a stronger emotionally intelligent foundation. So, let's discuss some strategies for you as a parent to manage responses in your teen that may trigger some of your underlying emotions.

❖ **First, you have to WANT to control your emotions.**

Too often, we take the same path of angry reactions with our family members that we do with people outside our homes. The attitude from parents that basically says, 'How dare you speak to me that way!' or 'I brought you in this world, I'll take you out!'. The problem in taking that stand is it may make you feel better for the moment, especially if you get your teen to back down and go to their room. But please hear me well when I say, you will pay the price for your emotional outburst and negative, angry responses. They may back down, but you will destroy something precious between you and your child.

❖ **Remember... you are talking to a CHILD, not another adult.**

I know that sometimes things can come out of the mouth of a teen that makes you want to take them out. I feel your pain. I remember one occasion when my eldest was 16; I got so angry with her that I put my hands around her throat in anger. There was no excuse for such a reaction from me. I was her mother. I had the responsibility of managing that situation and getting things back to a manageable situation, no matter what she said or did. I lost control, and she and our relationship paid the price. Because I did not know how to manage such situations, my eldest and I spent years with contention between us.

You are the parent. *You* have to manage high tension situations. You can't say whatever you feel like saying just because you are the parent. Whatever they see in you is the way they will learn to deal and respond. When you see behaviors and responses you don't like, realize that it is your responsibility to help them understand why the behavior is unacceptable and how the negative behavior will invariably undermine their potential and success. Look in the mirror before you respond in kind and lash out in emotionalism. They could very well be emulating the behavior they see in you.

❖ **Think before you open your mouth.**

When anger rises in your spirit, make the conscious choice to close your mouth and take a deep breath. That simple moment will lower your internal temperature. In the heat negative angry outburst, you will invariably say something you will regret. Once you say something harsh to a child, you can't take it back. You can apologize, but the words will be out of your mouth and forever planted in the spirit of your child.

Remember that who your child will be is a direct reflection of who you have told them they are. Even in angry situations, you should speak life into your child. Reinforce who you want them to grow to be; what God has created them to be. Don't speak death to their sense of self-confidence and expectations in a moment of angry outbursts.

Take a few moments to collect your thoughts before you open your mouth. If they continue to lash out at you, use your authoritative voice, not your angry one. In a loving tone, tell them you love them, but command them to calm themselves down. Be advised… this is not an easy task and won't immediately be natural for you if you are used to responding in anger. If you need to have them go to their room or a different part of the house until you can both talk in a calmer place, do so.

❖ **Once you are both in a more rational place, address the elephant.**

When you are both in a place to talk rather than shout or yell, talk about 'why' the situation made you upset; don't use the word 'anger'. In the mind of a teen, it seems to make them think of displeasure or disappointment in them. The goal is to get to a place of engaging conversation, not make them close up again. Ask them to explain in a calm voice why they were so upset.

Let them know you really want to understand where they are coming from. Listen to them without interruption until they finish making their point. Clearly explain any concerns you have without judgment or making your teen feel that they are not making smart choices. At this stage, the goal is to get them to talk to you more openly, not shut you out permanently.

❖ **Don't blame your child for your temperament.**

Remember, no one can make you do anything you don't want to do unless they are threatening your life or livelihood. So, your child cannot *make* you angry. They can't make you respond with angry outbursts. They may well cause you to feel anger, but how you chose to respond or react is your choice. Don't blame them. Don't tell them they made you say mean things; they made you do cruel things; they made you hurt them or humiliate them.

If you do such things, you need to find out why you respond in such negative ways; and if needed, get help so that your family does not pay for your out of control anger. Blaming your child for your issues is no different than your child blaming someone else for their problems. They, at least, have an excuse: they are young and haven't learned better. You, on the other hand ...have no excuse.

❖ **Take a timeout when the temperature rises.**

Timeouts aren't just for kids. High emotionally intelligent individuals understand their emotional triggers, and they have learned how to control their responses. They are able to read the emotional environment around them, and as a result, know how to de-escalate potential highly charged emotional conditions. Sometimes, that means as a parent, you may have to take a moment to get yourself in hand. Give yourself a timeout! Give yourself time to be able to be able to deal with the situation. When the situation gets tense, and you feel you may lose control, take a moment to breathe, calm down, and focus so you can deal without irritation or negative anger.

❖ **Stick with 'I' statements.**

As simple as this strategy is, it is one of the most important strategies you can use to manage a tense situation. Minimize *'you'* statements to minimize the perception of criticism and blame. Statements such as *'you made me angry,' 'you should not have done...'* or anything that suggests pointing the finger causes walls to go up, and people will respond defensively. Instead, try to focus on 'I' statements to describe problems when you talk to your child.

Be kind, loving, and specific. For example, rather than say, *"you never do the chores I tell you to do,"* try, *"It is upsetting when the instructions I give for chores are not completed. It's important that we all do our part for the household."* It's a subtle difference. But the verbiage can be the difference between a teenage rolling of the eyes (a norm, so expect it) and arguing based on a perceived attack; or them listening to what you have to say, even if it's with a heavy sigh.

❖ **Don't hold grudges.**

When an argument is over, allow your love for your child to outweigh your anger, frustration, or other negative emotion. Forgiveness is a powerful tool and has to be the cornerstone of any loving relationship. It is critically important in your home and with your children to employ forgiveness often. If you allow anger and other negative emotions to over-shadow positive feelings, it will result in a contentious relationship rooted in resentment and bitterness. But if you can forgive, you both might just learn from the situation and strengthen your relationship.

Forgiveness, according to the Bible, is so much more than mere words to pacify a situation. The word forgive literally means to 'send away,' 'depart,' or 'yield up.' So, to forgive means you are ready to release the situation, bury it, never to bring it up again. If you continue to bring the situation up means that you are stuck in a position of being offended and have not truly forgiven. As a parent, you cannot hold onto arguments and must master the art of forgiveness in order to be able to ensure you can help your child succeed. In turn, you will teach them a skill for life-long success and joy-filled living.

When Your Teen Loses It

The strategies above will help you maneuver the maze of uncontrollable anger and signs of low emotional intelligence. As an adult, that is your responsibility. However, your child will need help maneuvering the anger maze as well. When they show signs that negative emotions are taking control, as a parent, helping them calm their nerves is also your responsibility. There are several paradigms that can trigger extreme emotional responses in teens and adolescents. Below is a summary of the most common underlying factors:

❖ **Bullying from Peers** - Teens and adolescents who experience bullying on a regular basis will experience social isolation, anxiety, feelings of seclusion, fear, and other negative image issues that can become debilitating. Teens generally do not have the coping skills to deal with these feelings. Thus, they lash out when they feel overwhelmed.

❖ **Depression** - This is a major problem with teens and adolescents because unrecognized or untreated, it can have fatal outcomes. The National Alliance on Mental Illness reports that 20% of people experience depression during their teen years. In many instances, these cases have resulted in the growing and alarming trend of teen suicides. Some causes of depression in teens and pre-teens include extreme trauma; family conflict; sexual, physical, or mental abuse; loss of a loved one; medical issues with the child or a family member. One of the primary symptoms that's

84

often missed is the youth losing interest in all activities or withdrawing from things they use to find fun and enjoyable.

❖ **Grief** - Anger is one of the five stages of grief in normal situations. Thus, it is only natural for a teen who has lost someone dear to them to feel anger. Unfortunately, like some adults, some get stuck in their grief; and will exhibit angry outbursts or depression when they get stuck. They need a loving, strong parental or guardian influence to help them cope and move through the process.

❖ **Low Self-Esteem** - Generally, the result of poor self-image due to feelings of inadequacy in some areas of development, i.e., negative self-perceptions or self-image, weight issues, bad acne, school/sports performance. Circumstances involving rejection, criticism, or abuse can also contribute to low self-esteem.

❖ **Unresolved Family Conflict** - Major family conflict or drama, such as divorce, abuse, or death of a loved one, can leave teens and adolescents feeling hopeless. Some will even find ways to blame themselves in situations such as divorce or physical or sexual abuse. These situations are crippling for an adult; needless to say, teens and pre-teens are definitely not equipped to deal with such issues without help and guidance. Some will act out and behave in unhealthy ways.

❖ **Anxiety** - In the normal teen world, worry is a norm, i.e., grades, friends, popularity, dating, family issues, and a gamut of other situations can be nerve-racking for them. But when anxiety becomes excessive, it will interfere with a teen or pre-teen's ability to function or achieve desired goals. Teen anxiety disorders are among the most common mental health diagnosis among adolescent youth, resulting in excessive amounts of worry, fear, tension, or nervousness. The exact causes of teen anxiety disorders are unknown. However, the factors that impact have been attributed to genetics, brain chemistry, life stressors, and difficult home situations. Parents or guardians must be observant when symptoms of anxiety become so prevalent that they cause concern.

When to Seek Help

Learning to manage anger is a challenge for most adults. It is definitely a struggle for children of any age. Although anger in adolescents and teens is a norm, when you see signs that it is more than normal teen angst, as a parent, you will need to take some action to ensure the root cause(s) is identified and addressed so that your child can grow into a productive, successful adult. Anger is deemed problematic when the anger drives actions that become harmful or hurtful to self or others.

According to a study at Harvard Medical School, almost two-thirds of U.S. teens have experienced extreme angry outbursts such as threatening or engaging in some violent action at some time during their development. Of that number, almost eighteen percent have such outbursts on a regular basis. When outburst happen with such frequency, it is often a cry for help. Some of the red flags of problematic anger include the following:

❖ Getting into physical fights at school or at home with siblings on a regular basis.

❖ Excessive arguing and disagreements with parents, teachers, or other adult figures.

❖ Excessive arguing and dissension with other students, peers, or siblings.

- ❖ Extreme emotional outbursts, anger, and rage; verbal threats.

- ❖ Frequent irritability or moodiness.

- ❖ Irrational or illogical actions or behaviors.

- ❖ School or playtime bullying or purposeful intimidation.

- ❖ Relationship or dating violence, either as an abuser or a victim.

- ❖ Being cruel to younger siblings, pets, or other entities who can't defend themselves.

- ❖ Physical violence or destruction of property.

- ❖ Inflicting self-harm, i.e., cutting, burning, bulimia, etc. - this is a symptom of depression.

If you notice any of these signs in your adolescent or teen, you need to seek professional help, such as a counselor, pastor, or mental health practitioner. No matter the economic situation, there is help available. If you don't have a family practitioner or such services through an employer, a school counselor can help you identify a source of help. Don't allow parental shame or embarrassment to keep you from getting help for your child. If there are behaviors as described above something is wrong. In order to help position them for success in school, and as they become adults, they need you to do what they cannot do for themselves. They need you to get them help.

CHAPTER 6
SCHOOL RESOURCES PIPELINE

"A teacher inspires a child to reach academic success. A parent inspires their child to use that success to change the world." Unknown

School issues and hassles can often be avoided when parents know what's going on at school and understand what's going on with children at school. As a parent, you don't have to know the schoolwork that your child is learning, but it is advisable to understand the school and teacher's expectations so you can align to impress the expectations to the child at home. There will be times when a child may need something extra to be successful.

When you notice something is not quite going as expected, or other issues arise concerning a child's capacity to meet expectations, know that the school probably has resources that can help resolve the issues, especially related to what's going on in school. The keys are that you must be present and know when your child needs help, and you must have a collaborative relationship with your child's teacher for the good of your child.

Be Present – Stay Plugged In

Although I tried to know the names of my children's teachers, I was not as present for all of them as I could have been. In relationship development, we hear a lot about 'being present and in the moment.' But what does 'being present' mean, and what does it look like for a parent? Contrary to popular saying, human beings **cannot** multitask on a long-term basis. I was definitely a self-proclaimed multi-tasker until God helped me clearly understand that what I was doing was superficially completing tasks but was not giving any of those tasks my very best.

The human mind is an amazing organ, capable of retaining and processing massive amounts of information. However, it is only capable of truly focusing on one critical task at a time. When people try to multi-task invariably, something will be missed. The bottom line is that multitasking is the first killer to being present and making yourself wholly available for the things most important to you. Trying to perform several activities at one time results in an increased likelihood of missing critical information due to distractions and lack of attentiveness. So, how do you ensure that you are 'present' for your child?

First, recognize that you can only do one thing at a time when you want to do it well, and you must make doing parenting well your top priority. So, when your child enters the room or asks to speak with you, **STOP MULTI-TASKING!** That means turn the cell phone volume down; turn away from the computer; close down the laptop. I promise you that the world won't end while you speak with your child.

Being present simply means that for the moment in time that your child (or any loved one) is in your presence, asking for your time at that moment, your total focus is them. They have your undivided attention. In this fast-paced, rushed society we live in, we seem to fear that if we are not constantly plugged in to technology that we will miss something. But please hear me well: of all the things you might miss, don't miss an opportunity to connect to and hear the heart of your child. You will live to truly regret it if you do.

With my eldest, I knew the teachers but fell victim to listening to them more than I listened to my child. After all, they were the educators and knew what needed to be done, right? The critical thing is they do know education, but they don't know your child... you do. With my eldest, I listened to everything the teachers said when something was not going well. However, I made the detrimental mistake of not asking for my child's input. I never really talked to my child nor truly engaged in being present to listen to what they had to say. As a result, I openly acknowledge that I did not really know my *own* child. By the teen years, this resulted in feelings of deep-seeded resentment. I had a teenager who felt that I was not interested in understanding their side of any story. Although it was absolutely not true, it was how they felt. This impacted every area of our relationship well past the teen years.

When my 2nd born was a pre-teen, there was an accident that resulted in a special need. As a result, it was mandatory that I was involved in the special needs planning process. However, I was so focused on the special need issues, that I failed to truly engage in listening to my child's needs as a person. This resulted in my child connecting with elements that were not in their best interest by the time they reached the teen years. My desire was to be a good parent and ensure the educational process was as fair as possible to a special needs student. However, I failed to understand that my child was not only a student with a special need, but just as importantly, a person who still needed to be heard. Again, it resulted in issues that prevailed well past the teen years.

I was much more active with my youngest child's journey and had learned how to truly 'be present.' I learned from my mistakes and employed strategies that have proven to work in laying a solid foundation for success. In *being present*, I was able to tune in when things were not going well and take parenting actions even when no words were said. As a result, as a teen, we were able to talk about problems and issues as they arose and collaboratively get to places of resolution. Today, this foundation shows clearly in how much stronger this child is in seeing the positives over the negatives, and in boldly pursuing personal and professional goals.

The one clear lesson in helping position your child for success is **you must be present for your child.** You must also understand that every child's educational journey is a 3-prong journey. It involves three entities – parent, child, and teacher. As the parent, you are the key to assuring that the three components are aligned on one accord to make success happen for your child. You must be consistently present and aware of what's going on with your child; ensure the teacher knows you are available to help in any way needed and open to working collaboratively for the good of your child; and actively listen to hear what your child has to say, even when they don't know how to verbalize what they feel. This foundation positions you and your child well to have a successful school year every year.

Kick It Off Right

The start of a new school year is a huge event in the life of your child. You see it in the excitement of their voices when they talk about what the new year might be. You see it in them stressing over what to wear the first day of school. And hopefully, you hear it when they talk to you incessantly about what happened the first day. So, it is amazing that except for trying to figure out how to pay for school supplies and clothes, most parents take a completely hands-off approach to actually being a part of the excitement.

The best way to kick off a new school year is to begin by releasing the misconception that education is only the educator's responsibility. The new school year is not just a new school year for your child; it is also a new school year for you and your family. So, make sure you kick it off right for all of you. Below are strategies to help make it happen.

❖ **Don't Skip the School Orientation!**

School orientation is the day for you to go with your child to meet the teacher (s), get the class schedule, take a tour of the school, obtain the supply lists, and potentially meet some of the school administrators. This process is critical to beginning a collaborative, cooperative relationship with your child's teacher as well as administrative staff.

For younger children, participating in the orientation can alleviate some of the anxiety related to the new school year because they will know where their classes are, and they will have an opportunity to see their parent (the most important person in the world to them) engage with their teacher (the most important person in the school for that year). Overall, attending orientation benefits everyone. Children release some anxiety about the new school year; the teacher has an opportunity to meet you and understand your expectations of the year, and you will feel more at ease about who is teaching your child and what they expect of your parenting support role.

❖ **Get to Know the Teacher.**

Once you know who your child's teachers are, and you have the chance to meet them at the orientation, take steps to solidify the relationship. Remember, they meet a slew of people at the orientation, and the names and faces likely run together after a while. So, send a friendly email to reintroduce yourself and your child with the following information:

- Tell them how excited you are to be working with them to help your child succeed in the coming year.
- Include any special things you think they need to know about your child. Remember, they know education, you know your child.
- Let them know when is the best time to contact you if they need to do so.
- Remind them of some of the expectations you have of the coming year.
- If you can volunteer for anything, let them know what you can do to help them be successful in teaching the class that your child will be in.
- Ask about their expectations of you for the coming year and if there are things you need to know to position your child for success in their class.
  - Do they have any tips for homework or at-home learning?
  - How much homework will they generally give students?
  - What are the classroom rules and expectations? (So, you can reinforce them at home)

❖ **Be Jointly Collaborative with Older Kids.**
- If your children are older, they will have multiple classrooms and teachers. Make a point of introducing yourself to each of them, covering the same points as outlined in #2.
- Once you have a copy of their schedule and the classes' syllabi (each teacher will generally send a course

syllabus for review), sit down with your child to look it over to ensure you both are clear on the expectations of each class and any special projects on the horizon. Make copies for yourself. Your child should keep the original.

- Advise them to be who they are, not to fear being different and a strong individual. Strongly encourage them not to be followers or people pleasers. Let them know that no matter what goes on at school, you are available, and you've got their backs.

- They are older children, but they are still children. During the summer, it is likely that they veered way off of their normal sleep schedule. At least two weeks before school begins, usher them back to a sound sleeping schedule, so they are rested and ready for a strong school year.

- Remember that teens still need you. Make sure you go to orientation with them to show your engagement as they are elevated to their next level. Invite them to ask questions of the teachers as you meet them.

❖ **Start the Year Off with Positivity.**

- Don't just start with a positive attitude; keep that attitude throughout the year.

- Attitude is infectious. If you pour positivity into your child, as simple as it sounds, they will be more likely to take it with them throughout the day.

- The caveat is this: you cannot be positive each morning before school, but yell, rant, rave, and be critical at other times. You must be positive with your child much more than you are negative or critical.

❖ **Stay Away from Drama.**

▪ The bad thing about school is that there will be drama because so many people enjoy negativity, issues, and mess; some students will actually thrive on it.

  - School drama can take on many forms, from the silly and frivolous (who's dating who) to the serious and life-changing (school bullying).
  - Many people allow themselves to get sucked in without realizing it, and can become part of a bigger problem.

▪ Talk to your child about all potential negative paradigms that are impacting issues in today's society on school campuses.

  - Talk about teen dating violence, school bullying, the 'mean girl' paradigm, etc.
  - Let them tell you their views, and what they have seen and observed. Listen to what they say.
  - Talk openly and honestly so they understand the negative impact of these situations, how to respond if they are victims, and what to do if they are witnesses.

▪ Encourage your child to avoid the drama, drama makers, bullies, and those who put others down. Impress upon them the coolest people on the campus are not the self-professed 'cool kids,' but are really those who stand for what they believe in as well as stand up for those who may not have the confidence or strength to stand up for themselves.

▪ Remind them that their primary job is to do well in school; so, they are in school to learn, not bring drama, nor participate in it.

▪ Drama, in the form of anything other than a performing arts class, undermines a successful educational journey. A focus on drama is a set up for failure in everything else.

❖ **Form School-Happy Habits.**

From day one, implement a routine that is both conducive to an "early to bed - early to rise" schedule and one that is manageable for your family. Consider some of the following:

- Pack backpacks and lunches the night before the school day.
  - Ensure that homework and any due projects are in the backpacks.
  - If the project is too large for the backpack, put the project in a place that is close to the backpack.
  - Have a designated place for backpacks for easy pick up when it's time to leave.
- Set clothes out in the evening for the next day to ensure that items are clean, clothing items are coordinated, socks match, and shoes can be found.
- Stress the importance of a nutritious breakfast to maximizing learning potential.
  - If they will eat breakfast at home, ensure they get dressed before they eat so, they are ready to roll as soon as they finish eating.
  - If they will eat at school, ensure they understand what 'nutritious' means. Candy bars will not do!
- Schedule how the homework schedule will be managed. Plan to make time to be involved in the homework process if nothing more than getting them started on the work to be done.
- Set the expectations for homework strategy to ensure the children understand the importance of getting

homework done and that doing it at the last minute is not acceptable. Post the expectations so they can continuously see them and know your expectations.

- Review the next day's schedule with the family (another family bonding opportunity), either at dinner time or preparation for bedtime.

- Create a '*head to bed*' routine for the entire family. This will be a time that will announce its time for the family members to begin their wind-down routine to prepare for rest.
  - A '*Head to Bed*' routine will prompt everyone to get showers and baths, get into PJs, last call for snacks, read time, then bed.
  - This is advantageous for all kiddos as well as parents.

Implementing any of these strategies will set your child and the family up for a phenomenal school year. If you dare to implement them all, your child will truly be positioned to succeed; and you will enjoy the ride on the educational journey as well.

Collaboration Challenges

Ensuring you have a collaborative relationship with your child's teacher from the beginning is important. You will definitely want to contact your child's teacher and have a discussion if any of the following issues arise:

- ❖ Your child refuses to do assignments, even though you've tried hard to get him or her to do them.
- ❖ Homework instructions are unclear.

❖ You can't seem to help your child get organized to finish the assignments.

❖ You can't provide needed supplies or materials.

❖ Neither you nor your child can understand the purpose of assignments.

❖ The assignments are often too hard or too easy.

❖ The homework is assigned in uneven amounts. For instance, no homework is given on Monday, Tuesday, or Wednesday, but on Thursday, four of your child's teachers all make big assignments due the next day.

❖ Your child has missed school and needs to make up assignments.

❖ Your child seems to be losing interest in school.

❖ Your child is complaining about school, assignments, classmates, or some other aspect of his or her education.

❖ In some cases, the school guidance counselor may be helpful in resolving some of the issues above. Your child's teacher will know when the counselor is needed.

Open Communication Channels

Communication between teachers and parents is very important in resolving issues or concerns related to your child's education. Here are some guidelines in assuring that you forge an open line of communication with your child's teacher:

❖ Talk with teachers early in the school year. Get acquainted before problems arise, and let teachers know that you want to be kept informed. In this environment where many parents are too busy to get involved with their child's education, your child's teacher will not know you are an engaged parent until you let him or her know. Most elementary schools and many secondary schools invite parents to come to parent-teacher conferences or open houses. If your child's school doesn't provide such opportunities, call the teacher to set up a meeting.

❖ Contact the teacher as soon as you suspect your child has issues with the school or homework assignments. You should also and expect the school to keep in touch with you if there are issues. Schools have a responsibility to keep parents informed, and you have a right to be upset if you don't find out until report-card time that your child is having difficulties. However, if you stay engaged in your

child's education, you will likely realize that a problem exists before the teacher does. By alerting the teacher, you can work together to solve a problem in its early stages.

❖ As soon as you feel cause for concern for whatever reason, don't hesitate or delay in contacting your child's teacher. Request a meeting to discuss your issues and concerns. Tell the teacher briefly why you want to meet, ensuring that you stress your concern for your child and his or her educational success. Parents for whom English is a second language may need to make special arrangements, such as including another bilingual person.

❖ Your primary goal in interacting with your child's school is to forge a good working relationship with your child's teacher. Remember, it will take both of you to ensure your child's success. To that end, when you have concerns, go to the teacher first. Don't go to the principal without giving the teacher a chance to work out the problem with you and your child. It's the teacher who will have daily interaction with your child. That interaction should be a positive one for your child, you, and the teacher. You will risk damaging the relationship if you don't give the teacher an opportunity to resolve the issues.

❖ Approach the teacher with a cooperative, engaging spirit. Approach the collaboration with the belief that the teacher wants to help you and your child, even if you disagree about something. It's hard to solve problems if teachers and parents view each other as enemies. In such situations, the child is the one who will suffer.

❖ If you have a complaint, try not to put the teacher on the defensive. For example, avoid saying that you think the assignments are terrible, even if you think so. You might say, *"I'm glad Danny is learning to add and subtract in the first grade, but he is having trouble with the math worksheets. Is there any other way for him to learn the same material?"* This might encourage the teacher to try another approach, not only for your child, but also for the rest of the class, such as learning addition and subtraction by moving around buttons, sticks, or shells.

❖ Although teachers don't have time to tailor homework to the individual needs of each student, most teachers want to assign homework that children enjoy and can complete successfully. They welcome feedback from parents. So, let your child's teacher know how your child responds to what's going on in the classroom as well as to homework assignments, especially if they find it too hard or too easy, and even when your child finds an assignment particularly exciting. Teachers like to know when they've hit the mark and students are excited about a learning experience.

Communicating in Writing

A child's educational journey involves a constant need for parents to communicate with the school in some way. The primary communication strategy will, and should, generally involve verbal communication between the parent and the teacher. This can be a phone call or a collaborative email. However, there will also be times when communication needs to be more formal as in the form of a written letter.

❖ Letters are advisable if you feel that something needs to be documented to ensure that detail is not overlooked. A letter may be needed if you want to ensure that the teacher is aware of something critical in the home environment that might negatively influence the classroom dynamic. A verbal conversation is still advisable, but the written communication ensures a formal notification has been given.

❖ If there have been any disciplinary issues or other problems in the classroom, a letter with the agreed-upon actions by the teacher and the parent is a good way to ensure that what you understood as the agreed-upon strategy is also what the teacher understood. If, after reading your letter, the teacher feels that something is not as you understood it, another conversation can quickly and clearly address the disconnect.

❖ A letter might also be advisable if there are any medical instructions a teacher might need to know in case a medical emergency arises in the classroom.

❖ Letters provide both you, the teacher, and the school with a record of ideas, concerns, and suggestions. Letters give people the opportunity to go over what's been suggested or discussed. A lot of misunderstandings between parents and teachers can be avoided by writing down thoughts and ideas, reading over before sending it to the school or teacher. Each letter you write will be different depending upon the situation, whether you are sending it to the teacher, counselor, or administrator, and the issues being discussed.

❖ As a parent, your child's teacher or school administrator is not expecting you to write like a scholar. Just make sure your thoughts and ideas are written clearly. Although there is no expectation that the letter be perfect, do try to check your letter for correct spellings. You can do that if you type in on the computer with a spell check. If you are writing by hand, and you are not a spelling guru, keep a dictionary handy. You want to ensure that when your letter is read, the reader can understand what you are trying to say, and that they don't have to try to 'figure out' your message.

❖ Don't let your message get lost in wrong spelling, extremely poor grammar, and emotionalism. You are your child's advocate in their education. When you need to put concerns or problems in writing, do so in a factual, non-emotional, and businesslike way. This is how you will ultimately get the results you want for your child.

What's In Written Communication

Just remember that although the letter you are writing is personal to you, it is still a business letter.

❖ When writing any business letter, it is important to employ the K.I.S.S. rule – Keep It Short and Simple. Be sure you are clear on the purpose of the letter and what you want to relay.

❖ Ask these questions:
  ▪ Why are you writing the letter?
  ▪ What are your specific concerns?
  ▪ What are your specific questions?
  ▪ What would you like to see as a potential solution?

- What kind of feedback is desired, i.e., a written response, a meeting, a phone call, etc.?

❖ Each letter you write should include the following basic information:

  - Always date your letter.
  - Give your child's full name, your child's age and grade, the name of your child's teacher.
  - Summarize the special circumstances or situations that prompted you making contact.
  - State clearly what you would like to see as the next steps. Try not to include what is not desired; it will set a negative tone to the contact.
  - Provide your best contact information to include telephonic contact and email contact.
  - Keep the tone of your letter pleasant and businesslike.
  - Give the facts without letting anger, frustration, blame, or other negative emotions creep in.
  - Always end your letter with a "thank you.

Communication Success Tips

In any communication concerning your child's education, keep in mind that the ultimate goal is not to get YOUR way, but to ensure you get the best outcome for your child and his or her education. You will want to make a good impression so that the person reading your letter clearly understands your request and is more prone to say "yes" to your request. Remember, the person reading your letter may not know you, your child, or your child's situation. Following are some success tips:

❖ After you write your first draft, put the letter aside for a day or so. Then look at it again and revise it with fresh eyes. This will ensure that you catch potential errors in writing as well as the tone of writing.

❖ Read your letter as though you are the person who will receive and read it. You may also want to read it out loud. I'm a writer, and I find that reading what I wrote out loud helps me hear how others will read it.

   ▪ Is your request clear and concise?

   ▪ Are all relevant and important facts included?

   ▪ Is the tone professional and businesslike, with minimum emotionalism?

❖ If time permits and you know someone with strong communication skills, have them read over the letter to assess if your content is as clear and understandable as you think it is. If not, trust your review process.

❖ Use spell check and grammar check on the computer to ensure that errors are minimized.

❖ Keep a copy for your records.

Notification of Medical Condition

When your child has a medical condition for which care may be needed during the school day, it is important that the teacher and school administrators understand your child's condition, any medical regimen that's needed, and what they can do to help if something happens. In addition to having a verbal conversation, preferably face to face, you should document everything in writing.

❖ You may want to consult with your child's doctor in case there is something special that he or she might suggest for school personnel. A medical notification letter should include the following:

- Child's Name and Teacher
- Name of Child's Condition
- What the school needs to know about the child's condition
- Any situation that could trigger the condition
- Child's general limitations (physical, cognitive, etc.); or limitations if condition is triggered
- Any accommodations that may be needed, such as extra time to finish tests
- Medications your child is taking
- What to do in an emergency
- Feelings or symptoms your child may experience

❖ Encourage your teacher to treat your child as they would any other child. You want to ensure that your child's medical condition does not define your child, nor do you want your child to feel disconnected from the class.

❖ Ensure that you provide copies of the letter for your teacher, school nurse, counselor, and school administrators. Don't assume that if you send a letter to the teacher, everyone who needs to know will get a copy. That's your responsibility.

❖ In case of a change of teachers or school personnel, be sure that they are provided with the medical information. If anything changes with your child medically, be sure to update the information with school personnel.

Address Student Concerns

Although no parent wants to think in terms of potential issues with your child in school, the reality is there may be times when issues arise. Sometimes it will be your child that's the issue;

sometimes it will be something or someone else. Either way, you must remember, you are your child's greatest advocate in helping maneuver out of the issues so you, the child, and the teacher can focus on education. The following strategies will help you maneuver:

❖ **_Schedule to meet with the Teacher – with Open Mind_**
When you meet with your child's teacher to address specific concerns, be as positive and collaborative as possible. While meeting with the teacher, explain what you think is going; keeping in mind that your child's side of the story may not be the whole story. Sometimes a child's version of what's going on will differ from the teachers. For example, your child may tell you that the teacher never explains assignments so he or she can understand them. But the teacher may tell you that your child isn't paying attention when assignments are given.

Many parents don't want to accept that their child may not be as forthright and honest as they hope. But remember, children do sometimes stretch the truth. Additionally, you may not want to take the teacher's word as gospel automatically; not all teachers are 'teacher of the year.' However, remember your child's teacher exercises a lot of clout in your child's future. So, you do want to be open to all possibilities when you approach a discussion with your child's teacher.

The bottom line is that you will often have to be the mediator, making sure your child is positioned for success in the teacher's classroom. This means you will have to balance listening to your child, so they know you are present, and hearing the teacher out so he or she knows you are willing to collaborate.

❖ *Parent-Teacher Collaboration*

Be willing to compromise when and where needed with the teacher and with your child. Also, be as open and honest as possible with the teacher, to include if there are unfortunate family dynamics that can impact a child's capacity to learn, such as pending divorce, financial stress, family trauma, etc. They don't need to know all your detailed business, but they do need to know what may hinder success in the classroom.

Working together, there will likely be very few issues that you, the teacher, and other school resources will not be able to address and find some resolution. The strategy will depend on what the problem is, how severe it is, and the needs of your child.

- Is the homework often too hard? Maybe your child has fallen behind and will need extra help from a teacher, parent, or tutor to catch up.

- Does your child need to make up a lot of work because of absences? The first step might be working out a schedule with the teacher.

- Are there issues within the home affecting the child's ability or capacity to pay attention in class? If there are issues of not enough food at home, a difficult home environment (arguing, domestic violence, etc.), the school guidance counselor will be able to refer community resources.

- Does your child have or have been suspected of having a learning disability? If so, you'll need to get your child extra help, and the teacher may need to adjust some assignments. Some resources are listed in the Federal Sources section of this book.

107

- Does your child need extra support beyond what home and school can give? Ask the teacher, school guidance counselor, or principal if there are mentor programs in your community. Mentor programs pair a child with an adult volunteer who assists with the youngster's special needs, such as homework support, tutoring, or career advice.

Make sure communication is clear and that there is mutual understanding and agreement before the meeting ends with a plan of action to address problem areas. If, after the meeting, you realize you don't understand something, call the teacher to double-check and reconfirm the area of confusion. Always follow up to make sure that the approach and strategy that you and the teacher agreed upon is working.

CHAPTER 7
The Fatherhood Connection

"The best inheritance a father can give his children is a few minutes of his time each day." O. A. Battista

A father's positive and active involvement in a child's life is positively and compellingly correlated with a child's overall success in life. The outcome of a positive father-child relationship supports that the child will experience less depression and emotional distress, fewer expressions of negative responses such as fear and guilt, fewer conduct problems, less psychological distress, greater sense of social competence, higher levels of self-reported happiness, and fewer anxiety symptoms.

Children of involved, active fathers are more likely to demonstrate a greater tolerance for stress and frustration, have superior problem solving and adaptive skills. They will typically be more playful, resourceful, skillful, and attentive when presented with a problem. They are better able to manage their emotions and impulses in an appropriate manner. These research findings provide clear evidence that a father's positive connection to their child contributes significantly to a child's sense of happiness and their capacity to deal with life issues.

Absentee vs Non-Resident Fathers:

According to the Department of Health and Human Services' Promoting Responsible Fatherhood Initiative, a non-resident father is one who is not living with their child, but seeks to have an active role in their child's life no matter the difficulties. They are also referred to as non-residential or non-custodial fathers. These fathers may or may not have legal or physical custody of the child, but they are fully invested and committed to their child development and their successes.

An absentee father is a one who should be or could be in their child's life, but makes a conscious choice not to be. Although no reason that a father can produce is reasonable or sufficient for not being involved with their child, the absence may stem from several controllable paradigms. One of the most common reasons for the disconnect is the father who emotionally lacks empathy to understand the critical importance of their fatherhood role. He may be emotionally immature and afraid of the obligations of a father. The second paradigm is the father who is irresponsible and elects to simply ignore the fact that he is a father.

Another frequent excuse is the father who questions whether he is a child's father. Rather than pursue the truth, this father chooses to ignore his child altogether. An absentee father may also be a self-centered individual who just believes that his needs and desires supersedes the needs of a child or anyone else in his life. Finally, there is the father who may be connected to the child in some way, but is a workaholic and chooses work over spending time with his child. All of these are reasons that can be applied to a father's absence, but none are justifiable; and their absence has created an epidemic that negatively impacts a child's journey in education and in life.

Since 1965, the state of the family has taken a downward spiral. At that time, only 10% of all U.S. children, 18 years or younger, lived with a single parent. Today, more than one in four fathers live apart from their children. This devastating development has resulted in numerous issues within the family, in communities, and in schools related to youth development.

The Changing Family Paradigm

For the most part, mothers tend to be more involved in the educational process of children than fathers, especially in two-parent households. However, with the shift in the family dynamics in this age, roles are not as defined as in the past.

❖ Fathers, like mothers, have multiple roles: provider, nurturer, protector, disciplinarian, teacher, and societal guide, etc.

❖ Even with the changes in how today's families look, mothers still assume more responsibility for child-rearing and educational support.

❖ This division of labor may be due in large part to the fact that men continue to earn more than women in the labor force, as well as some prevailing pressures of societal expectations.

The rise in divorce rates and increase in children born out of wedlock has resulted in more children being raised in single parent households. It is estimated that at least half of all children today will spend some time in a single-parent home before they reach age 18. In most cases, this single parent will be the mother, although the proportion of custodial fathers is progressively increasing. In these single-parent homes, the lone parent must generally fill all roles within the family, meet all a child's basic and supportive emotional needs, and ensure financial needs are met as well.

The extent of a father's involvement with a child changes as children grow older and whether the child is a boy or a girl.

Regardless of the child's age, studies support that fathers are likely to be more involved with their son than they are with their daughter. As explained earlier, parents generally spend less time with their children as the children grow older, which means fathers who are not in the home will statistically spend even less time with older children.

Even though children may spend less time with their fathers, the importance of fathers to children's development does not decrease as a child gets older. It actually increases as the child ages. As a result, the research supports that a father's presence in a child's life is critical for different reasons at different ages. As such, a father's value to his child's emotional and educational journey must never be minimized. To that end, it is important that mothers do not prohibit non-resident fathers staying connected to their child. If there is contention between mother and father, parents need to get over it. The good of the child MUST be the overriding factor.

Recommendation to Reconnect

Whatever the family dynamic, a father's positive presence and influence in a child's life lays a strong foundation for educational and lifelong success. Be it a result of divorce or the parents not being able to get along, a child's need for a father's presence has been proven to be critical to a child's development. It is, therefore, imperative that mother and father forge a collaborative partnership to 'share' the educational journey for a child's success. Following are some suggestions to help non-resident fathers chart a path that is focused on the good of the child:

❖ If possible, remain geographically close to the child's primary home. If not feasible, be sure to communicate with the child on a frequent basis to show an active interest in the child's daily activities. Technology makes that easy in this day and age, so don't make excuses.

❖ Be intentional about being actively involved in what is happening at school or with the child related to school matters. This includes parent-teacher conferences, school events, extracurricular activities, etc.

❖ If not in close proximity whereby you cannot be physically present in the child's school, talk to the child about particular school activities and communicate continuously with the primary parent to make collaborative decisions about what transpires in school.

❖ Never let emotionalism cloud your actions, decisions, or behaviors related to school or at school events. If there are differences of opinions or desires, keep the child's best interest at the forefront of discussions and decisions.

❖ Always put aside personal differences for school events or educational decision making. At school events, you don't all have to sit together, but as parents, you should be able to keep the mood light and focus on the best interest of the child. You don't want to embarrass your child!

These simple strategies will let your child know how much you value them, how much you value education, and that you want and expect them to succeed.

Fathers and Educational Success

In today's high divorce rates, more households are categorized as single-family homes, often with father's living outside the primary home of the child.

❖ Statistics support that one in three children in the United States live without their biological father.

❖ That equates to more than 24 million homes without the father. Those statistics are highest in minority homes.

❖ Research also strongly support that fathers are critical to a child's educational success journey.

A Father's Influence

Fathers have a positive impact on a child's life with influence not only in education, but also social development, emotional development, and a child's self-esteem. While research supports that a child benefits most from the father-child paradigm when the father is in the home, it is also highly beneficial for the child when the nonresident father is positively engaged with his child. That means that when a father is not in the home, his positive and consistent engagement with the child is critical for a child's educational and overall success.

❖ When parents divorce or when a child is born to a single parent, the child has to face many challenges in many areas of life. One of the biggest challenges is the fact that the child will not have daily contact with the father.

  ▪ The unfortunate reality is when the father is not in the home, without a targeted plan of action to stay connected, fathers tend to lose contact with their children over time. This generally has devastating emotional impact on the child.

  ▪ The primary impact of this failed connection is on the child's sense of self-esteem and self-value.

  ▪ Fathers who understand and value their roles tend to be more focused on staying connected to and involved with their children after divorce or separation.

  ▪ Maintaining the connection is good for fathers and children. However, for the emotional well-being of the child, it is imperative that the connection led to a strong positive relationship.

❖ Extensive research exists on the importance of parental involvement in children's education, with more recent research focused on the contributions of mothers versus fathers related to a child's educational process.

- Child psychologists are increasingly reaching the conclusion that a father's influence is not identical to that of mothers.

- The current focus and attention devoted to fathers is not intended to lessen the importance of a mother's influence. But rather to highlight the fact that fathers have a critically important role to play and must not delegate the educational journey to mothers only, especially when the father is not in the home.

- A father's positive presence in a child's life directly influences the child's perception of themselves and their environment.

- According to the research, effective father engagement and connection to the child encourages independence, standing up for oneself, self-acceptance, and self-worth.

- When fathers are available and involved with their children, both boys and girls perform better academically, and both boys and girls find greater value in who they are as individuals. This is the foundation for long term success in a child's life.

Impact of a Father's Absence

According to the U.S. Census Bureau, there are more than 24 million children in America whose biological father is not in the home or is completely absent from the child's life. That equates to one out of every three children who are living without a strong fatherly presence in their lives. It has been determined that the 'Father-Factor' is a major influence in most of society's negative impact issues facing America today related to children. The resulting statistics are presenting a real crisis in this country. It is imperative that fathers realize their critical influence on a child's behavioral and psychological development, and commit to being more involved, responsible, and dedicated to being present with and for their child. As outlined below, when a father is not there, statistics fully support that children suffer:

❖ Children whose father is absent are 6 times more likely to suffer neglect; 8 times more likely to suffer maltreatment; and 10 times more likely to be victims of sexual and physical abuse, largely due to the mother's live-in partner relationships.

❖ They are 5 times more likely to commit suicide; 32 times more likely to run away; 20 times more likely to have behavioral disorders.

❖ They are twice as likely to repeat a grade in school; 9 times more likely to drop out of high school; and for those who remain in school, they are less likely to make As.

❖ They are more likely to abuse drugs and alcohol. This is likely due to the ease with which fatherless children fall to the influence of others.

❖ Over 65% of children who live in homes without a father's presence live below the poverty line.

❖ Girls are 7 times more likely to become teenage mothers as they are statistically prone to sexual activity earlier.

❖ Boys are 20 times more likely to commit crimes and end up in prison.

These are just a few of the statistics that point to the high price children pay when a father is absent and has no consistent connection to their child during those formative and teenage years. It suggests a direct impact on the important work fathers do to help lay a foundation for success in their children's lives.

The absence of fathers in the home, or the inability of fathers to assume their role in the family, results in the alarming statistics that can truly increase the possibilities of potential failure in school and beyond. A landmark study by the U.S. Department of Education found that children in two-parent families and of non-resident fathers who were highly involved in their children's education were more likely to get mostly A's, embrace a positive mindset concerning the learning journey, and truly enjoy the school experience. The illustration below summarizes the findings of the study.

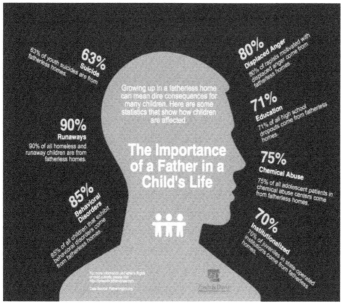

U.S. Department of Education

117

Even when fathers don't live with their children, it's clear that their involvement matters to academic achievement. It is up to the father to ensure that his absence does not result in any of the statistics above.

Absence Does Not Negate Being Present

There is nothing easy about being a father, especially when the father cannot be with his child every day. That means that if you are not in the home with your child, you will have to be more intentional and strategic about making a daily imprint on your child's day. In today's technology-driven society, quite frankly, you have no excuse for not 'being present' for and with your child.

As we discussed in chapter 6, being present means that you commit dedicated time and give your child your total focus and attention. As a non-resident father, you will have to schedule time with your child, and every moment you are with them or in connection with them, you need to be present. It means that if you schedule a check-in call, no matter what, you don't miss the call. Even if you have to call and speak for only a minute to tell them although you can't talk long, you want them to know how much you love them. No matter what, you need to be present on schedule. A five-minute call means more than you could ever imagine.

My father was never a non-resident father; he was an absentee father. He was never there, never available, and in my eyes never cared. Just hearing his name would bring tears to my eyes well into my teen years. Because of his absence, I was clueless as to what my value was when it came to relationships. I felt if my own father could not love me, I must not be worth much. That self-concept followed me in everything I did, everywhere I went. I did not have low self-esteem. I had no self-esteem, no sense of value, and no feeling of worth for well into my adult years.

My saving grace as far as education was concerned was my aunt and grandmother who would not let me underperform. However, they could not give me what I missed because of my absentee father. I lived a broken life for years because my father was not around to love and support me, nor was he there to protect me from someone who hurt me in my developmental years. For a long time, I hated him for his absence, and it affected so many areas of my life, to include how I dealt with and perceived relationships.

Children are not meant to live and grow without their father's presence and influence. To fully understand your role as a father, in addition to statistics, I must refer to God's commands and instructions to summarize the criticality of the role of a father. So many times, we fail to truly understand the implication of what the Bible says because we never study the context in which the instructions were given.

God's Word makes it clear that both parents must work together to raise children to be their best selves. However, no matter how Scripture is interpreted or misinterpreted, fathers have a driving role and responsibility in ensuring a child has what they need to become thriving adults. Here are some of the fundamental things God has to say about how critical fathers are to child development.

❖ **As a father, you are one of your child's first teachers.**

- Proverbs 22:6 says it is your responsibility to "train up a child in the way he or she should go."
- That means that a father's participation is critical to helping a child learn who they can potentially become.

- It is your responsibility in collaboration with the mother to teach your child what is right or wrong in life.

- If your influence is not in your child's life, a major source of motivation will be missing.

❖ **Fathers must spend quality time with their children and communicate well.**

  - Deuteronomy 6: 6-9 makes it clear that fathers must engage their children in the kind of deep, meaningful conversations that impart more than facts, but teach wisdom.

  - If you don't think you have wisdom to impart, fake it 'til you make it. Perhaps you need to expand who you hang around so you can help your child grow into who they are meant to be. Connect to men who have more experience than you have and learn from them; ask for advice and guidance.

  - You may not have thought about it, but you are an unconscious example of what your son will emulate and what your daughter will look for in a man. Children learn from what you do consistently, not just what you say

  - Schedule regular times to talk to your children and make those times count.

❖ **Fathers are to exhibit compassion for their children.**

  - Psalm 103:13 points out that a compassionate nature is important to a father's role.

  - Children may listen to what you say, but your actions speak more loudly than your words. They will do what they see you do. They learn by observing you.

120

- A big part of what they 'see' as a non-resident father is how you treat them. Every word they hear or don't hear, every broken promise, every perceived act that says you don't care is being recorded in their memory.

- It is critical in your role that each encounter with them be an example of compassion in action. They need to be on the front end of being a recipient of your kindness, benevolence, and compassion.

❖ **Fathers must never give up on their child.**

- The story of The Prodigal Son in Luke 15:20-24 is the story of a father who never gave up on his child, despite the child making some really bad decisions. When the child humbly returned, the father welcomed him with open arms.

- A good father can discipline, scold, and hold a child accountable, but they never give up on them.

❖ **Fathers should not provoke their children.**

- Ephesians 6:4 instructs that fathers should not provoke their children to anger. The implication here is that a father's unreasonable and severe actions should not push a child into feeling discouragement or raging anger.

- Colossians 3:21 commands that fathers should not exasperate (frustrated) their children and make them feel downhearted.

- If a non-resident father becomes an absentee father, the child will be discouraged, exasperated, and extremely angry.

- If the only words a child hears from a non-resident father are words of disappointment and reprimand, they will be greatly downhearted and hopeless.

- It is a father's job to encourage and give loving correction. This is even more critical for non-resident fathers.

❖ **Fathers are charged to pray for their children.**
  - In 1 Chronicles 29:19, David prayed fervently for his son, Solomon, that God keeps him and protects him.
  - Non-resident fathers should beseech God even more to protect their children so that God can constantly watch over them because their earthly father cannot be there constantly.
  - Even if they don't understand faith, children who know that their father prays for them daily have a deep sense of being loved and protected.

Almost any man can biologically father a child, but it takes intention and consistency to be a good father as defined by God. His desire for every child is to be all that they were born to be, and to be successful in their hopes, desires, and endeavors. It is hard for a child to see the fulfillment of God's vision for them when their earthly father is absent, not present, and chooses not to engage. Your child needs you to be available. Be the father that God designed you to be so that your children can be all that they are destined to be.

Father's Involvement in School

A father's involvement in a child's educational journey lays a firm foundation for a success mindset throughout life. Following are simple strategies a father can implement that will leave life-long impressions on the child:

❖ **Read to your child as often as possible.**

Children who learn to read well at an early age will develop a joy for reading and have more success in school.

- For younger children, read out loud with them regularly. If you are a non-resident father, buy or check out two copies of the same picture book. At bedtime or a time mutually agreed upon, read the book over the phone while the child enjoys the pictures and your voice.

- For older children, have them read the selected book and discuss it with them on the phone. Have them give their interpretations or thoughts about what they read. Let them know you value what they have to say. This will encourage appreciation of reading, critical thinking. and communication skills. It will also enforce a message from you that they are loved and valued, which enhances self-esteem.

- When possible, connect the reading material and topic to a school activity or assignment.

❖ **As your child ages, encourage them to ask critical questions.**

As long as they're respectful, allow your child to challenge you when you have discussions or reading time. I don't mean challenge as in challenging your authority as a parent. But allow them to discuss how they interpret something that is said or read, and why they are interpreting it differently from how you or others may interpret the information.

- Encourage them to defend their ideas and concepts. This will inspire them to learn to stand up for themselves in a respectful way; as well as teach them that their voice and what they have to say is important. This is definitely something you want to teach them, so they know how to stand up for what they believe when you are not around.

- This strategy will be invaluable not only as the child progresses to higher levels of education, but will also establish a relationship whereby your child will feel comfortable talking to you about any issues, problems, or concerns as they grow older.

- This is an essential suggestion for the primary as well as the non-resident parent.

❖ **In collaboration with the mother, set clear and achievable educational expectations.**

Statistics support that successful college students had parents who set expectations early and were clear about what they expected of their children. In collaboration with the mother, come to some agreed upon, realistic expectations. Without being overbearing, talk to your child regularly to set expectations to guide and support the path to success.

❖ **Learn your child's day-to-day routine and stay involved.**

Knowing your child's schedule, such as the timing of sports or lessons, will make it easier to connect to your child and maintain a collaborative relationship with the primary parent.

❖ **Minimize conflict between you and the mother.**

The advent of a divorce or situations involving unmarried parents will often be fraught with emotional issues and difficulties. Parents must remember, be mindful, and be determined in realizing that the issues are the parent's issues, **not the child's issue.**

- A well-adjusted child has the greatest potential of being successful in school, and subsequently in life.

- Emotional discord between parents must never spill over into how a child is treated nor the level of interaction with your child.

- The more you work to reduce conflict with your child's mother, the easier it will be to play an important, healthy role in your child's life.

- The healthier your role in your child's life, the easier it will be to maintain a focus on the well-being of your child, not your emotional irritations with the mother.

- Be VERY careful not to make your child a middle person amid adult mess and distress.

❖ **Coordinate parenting strategies with your child's mother.**

When a child has to spend time in two separate homes,

differences in parenting styles can be highlighted and differences magnified. In these situations, mothers and fathers may take vastly different approaches to discipline, rewards for the child, school expectations, home chores, or other responsibilities.

- Inconsistencies in the home environment of the parents can and will often leave a child confused and vulnerable to developing several behavioral or emotional problems.

- Continual inconsistencies in expectations can lead to problems in school, which will impact the journey to life's success.

- It is important to keep a healthy line of communication open between parents. As much as possible, have critical conversations to get on one accord concerning how responsibilities will be handled.

- This will also minimize the inevitable game of playing one parent against the other.

❖ **Don't be a 'Vacation' Dad.**

Non-resident fathers can sometimes get caught in the trap of being a source of entertainment for their children during the time they spend with them. Weekend visits can be so filled with trips to amusement parks, the zoo, movies, sporting events, etc. that no real parenting takes place. This can cause several significant problems.

- Being a 'vacation' dad can lead to a child's expectation that dad's house is the fun place to be, and 'home' (mom's house) is boring.

- This paradigm in expectations can become very expensive for dad and extremely frustrating for mom. This can be a major disconnect between you and mom.

- This can also easily lead to the child playing one parent against the other, which will never result in the most positive outcomes for the child.

- To eliminate this situation, both parents must keep an open line of communication to plan the time you spend with your child.

- Ensure the child has chores at your place as well as at their mom's place, and the 'fun' activities are split between you and mom.

- Ideally, although mom's house will be the primary 'home' for the child, as much as possible, create a home environment at your residence for your child as well.

❖ **Always affirm your love and support of your child.**

- Tell your child often how much you love them and believe in them.
- Let your words of affirmation and encouragement be the foundation of the message they consistently hear from you.
- Children need to know that their father is there to help them with their struggles.
  - Girls need you to be their knight-in-armor, knowing that if they are threatened, you will be there.
  - Boys need you to be their example of what being a man is all about, there to guide them when they are confused and lost.
- As a father, continually communicating your adoration and encouragement will help your child build a sense of security and confidence in all they do, from education throughout life.

I am the survivor of an absentee father. I promise you that you don't want to expose your child to the challenges and hardships your child will have to face if you are not present. Whether you succeed in doing all the activities suggested in this guide is not what's most important. What's most important is that you are willing to take the time to employ as many of these strategies as possible and make every effort to be the greatest advocate on your child's educational journey. As a father, what you do or don't do is significant and makes a huge impact. Your child needs you to be in their corner. Show them that you believe in the greatness of their potential; and that you will do whatever is needed to help them lay the strongest foundation to succeed.

CHAPTER 8
SPECIAL NEEDS PARENTING

"The strongest people are not those who show strength in front of us, but those who win battles we know nothing about."
Unknown

When parents initially learn that their child has a disability, the news is often met with a gamut of emotions from disbelief, anger, denial, and then, eventually, acceptance. Such devastating news is closely akin to the stages of grief someone feels when they experience death. However, once you accept the situation and learn the tenants of what's going on, the journey will be less traumatizing. Initially, parents may feel isolated, alone, and not know what to do. It is critical that parents do not isolate but open themselves to connecting to other parents of children with special needs and finding out what resources are available to ensure that their lives with their child is a joyous journey.

As the parents of a special needs child, when we were informed that our child would have special needs from an accident, there was not as much information or support as there is today. That was almost 20 years ago. We did not know or fully understand what taking the journey with a special needs child meant, nor did we have anyone to guide us down the path of understanding what our rights were as parents of a child with special needs. We had to learn as we traveled, which means we stumbled A LOT. Today, however, there is so much information readily available to ensure that parents are equipped with the tools to help them position their children for success in school and life.

Truisms About Special Needs Parenting

❖ **Parenting a child with special needs does not make you a superhero.** You will have moments when you lose patience, get tired, frustrated, and occasionally raise your voice. Don't expect so much of yourself that you stress yourself to the max.

❖ **Parents of children with special needs have insecurities.** There were many times when my son was young in school when I just did not know what to do. At the time, I felt that was unacceptable, and I did not want to admit that I did not know. Your job is to be knowledgeable. However, you will never know everything about your child's situation. Guess what, neither do any other parents. All you can do is make the best decision you can make with the information you have at the time. If you don't know what that is sometimes, it's okay.

❖ **(In spite of the bullet point above) Parents of children with special needs are experts on their own kids.** You don't have to be an expert on the disability that your child has. But be always present with your child, so that you know your child. Know your child's needs, what they like/dislike, what makes them happy, and what upsets them. If any specialist engages your child, you must be their voice.

❖ **Parents of children with special needs are no different than other parents.** You are a parent of a child who needs your love, support, care, and dedication. There are many different challenges that parents face with their children. As a parent of a child with special needs, you have an obvious challenge to deal with as a family. Other challenges of other parents may not be so obvious, i.e., belligerence, disobedience, drug addiction, self-esteem issues, etc. Don't isolate by differentiating your position as a parent from other parents.

❖ **Parenting special needs kids can be lonely and exhausting.** Parenting can be a lonely and exhausting journey, even for fully healthy, very obedient children. However, whenever there is a challenge, the journey can be more tiring and seemingly lonelier than is comfortable. These challenges bring heightened stress, long hours, and emotional fatigue. The key to being a successful parent to a special needs child is knowing when you need to rest and finding time and ways to destress. You will need time to rest and refresh. You may need to think outside the box to make it happen, but you must find a way.

❖ **Caring for children with special needs can be expensive.** Often these children have needs that require therapies, doctors, medications, etc. that can tap deep into the family's budget pocket. Although there may be help with some things, some other things are at the sole cost of the parent. That means parents of children with special needs must be strategic, tactical, and frugal to make it all happen. Parents of special needs kids are often deep in debt.

❖ **Sometimes parents with children with special needs can get defensive.** Some parents have had some bad past experiences with someone they encountered on their journey. Not all that they encountered were kind. Some kids can be cruel, so can some adults. When people don't understand a thing, those who are emotionally immature will ridicule. The parent of children with special needs have often had to be the shield to protect their child from the unkind. As a result, some have learned to be poised for the attack if needed. Although it can be difficult, it is important for parents to stay in a positive place and judge each person you encounter for what they bring to your child and your life.

Educational Journey for Special Needs Success

You are your child's first teacher, laying the foundation for what they believe they can and will achieve. You are their first and most critical role model. You must be their most vocal advocate. You are charged with ensuring that they get their needs met, they have a chance to succeed, and they get all that you desire in their education and life. Keep in mind that each teacher is only in your child's life for a season. You are their constant. You must be active and vocal in ensuring they have the best start possible in their education.

Parent of a child with special needs have two driving goals:

1. Ensure the school provides your child with a free appropriate public education that includes special education and related services designed to meet your child's needs and prepare them for further education, employment, and independent living.

2. To build a productive, healthy, respect-based working relationship with your child's school, teachers, and IEP professionals.

As your child's number one advocate, take ownership of becoming an expert about all that relates to your child's needs and the school's provision for those needs. Be mindful of the following:

❖ You must know the laws related to special needs programming and how your child's school deals with special needs programming.

❖ You must be conscientious in dealing with your child, understanding his or her condition, and being familiar with any change of laws or guidelines.

❖ It is hoped that your child's school is fully knowledgeable and compliant with special needs requirements. However, as an advocate, you must stand to be vocal if the school is not performing as required.

❖ Keep records of everything. Documentation is the key to success for most children, especially special needs children. Request copies of every IEP (Individualized Education Program) that is held. Document all meetings and discussions related to your child's education, to include telephonic conversations or quick meetings with teachers or school administrators.

❖ Don't be afraid to ask questions or seek clarification of what's discussed. Often special needs professionals will speak in their professional language, as do most professionals. IF something is said that you don't understand, stop the presses. Tell them you need them to break it down and make it clear. Make sure you understand how everything that is discussed applies to your child.

❖ You know your child better than anyone. If you hear something that does not sit well with you based on knowing your child, ask questions, define issues that you think maybe problematic. Your teachers are experts in special education. You are the expert in your child. If you align your expertise with your child's teacher and communicate from a foundation of respect, keeping the

132

interest of the child at the forefront of every discussion, your child will always win.

❖ Master the art of communicating and writing from a place of advocacy, and not one of emotionalism. As tiring and frustrating as some parts of your journey as a parent of a special needs child can be, remember you are your child's voice. Make sure your child's teachers, specialists, and school administrators listen when you speak. Make your ideas, comments, suggestions, and explanations clear and powerful. Emotionalism will undermine that strategy.

❖ Get two 3-ring binders and loose-leaf paper to keep track of all that transpires on your child's journey.

  ▪ The first is to include your research and information on your child's disability, condition, impacting legislation, etc.

  ▪ The second should include all information related to your child's school, IEPs, school meetings, and discussions, etc.

The Law of the Special Needs Land

As a parent with a special needs child, it is imperative that you know the laws that impact you, your child, and your educational journey as a family. Although most individuals and specialists will give you information when asked, you should not depend on others to tell you of your child's rights. Read for yourself. As the Bible says, study to show yourself approved, a workman who need not be ashamed. That simply means you should study and learn so you can be an authority on a matter in your own life. Herein are some of the major laws that directly impact your special needs child's educational journey.

Individuals with Disabilities Education Act (IDEA)

The Individuals with Disabilities Education Act (IDEA) is the federal special education law that ensures that children with disabilities are provided a free and appropriate public education, also called FAPE. Under IDEA, each state is required to develop guidelines on how special education services will be provided to children with disabilities. Under each state's guidelines, local school districts must develop policies to ensure each child receives the best education possible. Some states provide parents more rights and protections than are entitled under federal law. Therefore, it's critically important for parents to know the laws and provisions within their state.

Under IDEA, each child receiving special education services must have an Individualized Education Program (IEP). The IEP is a written document that the school and parents collaboratively develop based on the unique needs of the child. The IEP clearly outlines the child's needs and lists the services that he or she will receive.

Under IDEA, in order for a child to be eligible for special education, they must have issues in one of the following categories:

❖ A serious emotional disturbance.

❖ A learning difference.

❖ An intellectual disability.

❖ A traumatic brain injury.

❖ Be diagnosed on the spectrum of autism.

❖ Vision and hearing impairment.

❖ Physical disabilities.

❖ Developmental delays (including speech and language difficulties).

❖ Any other diagnosed health impairment that impacts learning.

Section 504 - Civil Rights Act of 1973

Section 504 in the Civil Rights Act (1973) stipulates that schools must not discriminate against children with disabilities and provide them with reasonable accommodations. It covers all programs or activities, whether public or private, that receive any federal financial assistance. Reasonable accommodations include untimed tests, sitting in front of the class, modified homework, and the provision of necessary services. Typically, children covered under Section 504 either have less severe disabilities than those covered under IDEA or have disabilities that do not fit within IDEA. Under Section 504, any person who has an impairment that substantially limits a major life activity is considered disabled.

Americans with Disabilities Act (ADA)

The Americans with Disabilities Act (ADA) (1990) requires all schools, other than those operated by religious organizations, to meet the needs of children with disabilities or disorders. Under the ADA, children who qualify cannot be denied educational services, programs, or activities; and it prohibits discrimination against all such students.

Evaluation of Your Child

As a parent, if you have any concerns about a potential disability with your child, you may request an evaluation of your child through your child's school to determine any needs for special education or related services. The evaluation may include psychological and educational testing, a speech and language evaluation, occupational therapy assessment and behavioral analysis. These are the steps you need to take:

❖ Meet with your child's teacher to share your concerns and request an evaluation by the school's child study team. Parents can also request independent professional evaluations.

❖ Submit your requests in writing for evaluations and services. Always date your requests and keep a copy for your records.

❖ Keep careful records, including observations reported by your child's teachers and any communications (notes, reports, letters, etc.) between home and school.

The results of the evaluation will be the determinant of your child's eligibility to receive a range of services under the applicable law. If qualifying disabilities are found, an Individualized Education Program (IEP) or a Section 504 Plan (the 504 Plan often less strict than an IEP) would be developed collaboratively between the school's specialist and you, as a parent.

Parents do not make the decision whether their child is eligible for services under the law. That decision is made by going through the evaluation process at the school level. Also, the findings of a school's evaluation team are not final. If you do not agree with the initial findings, you have the right to appeal their decision. The school is required to provide you with information about how to make an appeal. Additionally, you have the right to participate in the developmental plan for services that will be provided.

Remember, it is your job as a parent to take necessary steps to make sure your child receives the services he or she needs to ensure they have the best start in life possible. The process can be confusing and intimidating for parents, but here are just a few tips:

❖ Request copies of the school district's Section 504 plan or IEP guideline. This is especially important when a school district refuses services.

❖ If the school district does not respond to your request, you can contact a U.S. Department of Education Office of Civil Rights Regional Office for assistance.

❖ If the school district refuses services under the IDEA or Section 504 or both, you may choose to challenge this decision through a due process hearing. This is a legal hearing in which you and your child have an advocate who can help you present your concerns and requests.

❖ In extreme cases, it may be necessary to hire your own lawyer if you decide to appeal a school's decision and your research supports that your child's needs are not being met.

The IEP Process/Expectations

Once your child is determined to meet the guidelines for special services under disability statutes, your child's school will focus on preparing the IEP to lay the foundation for your child's success. You will be contacted to schedule the IEP. However, if you don't hear from the school, feel free to contact the school's counseling unit to get the ball rolling.

The IEP meeting will generally include five primary roles:

❖ The special education teacher – has knowledge on what forms of specially designed instruction can be facilitated in your child's school.

❖ The general education teacher – provides expertise in the general education curriculum of the grade in which your child is or will be placed.

❖ The district representative – will ensure that the IEP is legally compliant, and all the stipulations of the IEP are inclusive in the plan.

❖ The test data interpreter – to help the team understand the testing information and the implications of the test outcome on your child.

❖ You – with a unique understanding of who your child is.

While all five roles are required at an IEP meeting, it is possible for one member to serve more than one role. For instance, a special education teacher is generally trained to interpret test data. Thus, the special education teacher may serve both as the special education teacher and data interpreter.

It is critically important that you do not miss your child's IEPs. Your interest in your child's educational journey is a clear message to your child and all who interact with him or her that you believe in your child's potential to be successful despite the identified disability. Your child may or may not be in the IEP meeting. However, the older the child, the more you may want to consider including them in the IEP. Children age 16 and older are required to attend. Dependent upon your child's condition, other potential attendees to the IEP include a school psychologist, an adaptive physical education teacher, a speech/language specialist, an occupational therapist, or other specialized service providers.

What Goes into the IEP?

Every possible aspect of your child's capacity to learn and grow should be codified in your child's IEP. A good IEP is a very specific document that details the best strategy to position your child to succeed by maximizing his or her capacity with a special need. It is important to remember that **the IEP is a binding document for the provision of services between the school district and you as a parent.** This means that if a district does not provide services that are promised in the IEP, it is non-compliant with the IEP and the law. It does not mean that if a child has not made as much progress as the team would like to see, the teacher or district should be sued.

One of the biggest elements of the IEP that is not written in the plan is the mandatory collaboration with a strong foundation of respect between school representatives and parents. In other words, as a parent, you should do all you can to have a strong and close working relationship with your child's IEP team. According to the 'The Special Education Guide,' a comprehensive IEP must include the following:

❖ **Present Levels:**

▪ This is a snapshot of who the child is and how he/she is doing right now.

▪ This should include eligibility information, contact information for the parents, and a summary of current work.

▪ This summary should include data such as reading and math test results, current grades, observed skills, behavioral referrals, records of work habits.

- The summary should be specific. Teachers should avoid writing generalities or subjective comments such as 'Jimmy is well-behaved.'

- When preparing the summary, family and parental input should be obtained and included.

- In essence, the present levels of academic achievement and functional performance (PLAAFP) should state the student's strengths and weaknesses, classroom performance, and provide measurable baseline data from which goals are created.

❖ **Offer of Free and Appropriate Public Education (FAPE):**

- This is commonly referred to as 'placement' or 'services.' This is the binding part of the contract, in which the school district offers classroom or ancillary services such as speech therapy or adaptive physical education.

- It should specify how often (number of days in the school year) the child will receive these services and the duration of the services (how many minutes per session).

- This section cannot use variable terms, such as 'as needed' rather should spell out the minimum number and times for provision of services.

❖ **Goals:**

- Goals are written to provide measures of progress.

- Goals can be academic, behavioral, social, or transition-based, and must be written for areas of need. For example, if a student is far behind peers in reading, he or she should have a defined reading goal.

- Goals should be achievable (the team should agree that the student could reasonably meet the goal in one year) and measurable (the teacher must feel that he or she can provide hard data and work samples to show progress toward the goal).

❖ **Accommodations and Modifications:**

- Accommodations and modifications are changes to the classroom environment that may be necessary to assist the student.

- Teachers and parents are often unclear about the difference between an accommodation and a modification. The general rule is this:
  - If it helps the student to complete the same work at the same level as his peers, it is an *accommodation.*
  - If it changes the work, or the work is completed at a different level, it is a *modification.*
  - For example, allowing a child to type his notes rather than handwrite them is an accommodation. An adult typing them for him is a modification.

❖ **Transition Plan:**

- Recent legislation requires that students who will turn 16 within the life of the IEP must have a transition goal and plan.

❖ **Signature Page and Meeting Notes:**

- Each member of the IEP team typically signs, indicating that he or she was present at the meeting and approves the notes from the meeting.

- The parent must consent to the accommodations, modifications, and placement (offer of FAPE) from the school district for the initial IEP to be implemented.

What Happens at the IEP Meeting?

❖ Every year, the IEP team will meet for the Annual Review (AR) to assess the progress of your child's plan and where changes are needed. The AR is designed to assemble your child's IEP team to discuss the student's needs and performance by reviewing progress reports, new data, and test results.

❖ Every three years, the team will also meet to discuss the student's continuing eligibility for services. This meeting is called the Triennial Review (aka the 'Tri') and is usually combined with the AR.

❖ Team members should come to the annual meetings with a draft of their ideas to maximize the time for discussion and final decision making.

❖ The IEP meeting should not be the only time that teachers, parents, and other service providers discuss a child's progress. Remember that the IEP is a working document and can be modified and changed as needed throughout the school year. It is important to keep the line of communication open between team members and to continuously work together to best meet the needs of your child.

Take an Advocate Stance

Generally, you will find that most schools are very open to working with you as a parent of a child with special needs. As such, they will be responsive to your calls or request for help involving your child. If that proves not to be the case, remember you are your child's only real advocate. If you don't take a stand to get what they need, they likely won't get it. The guidelines below will help you manage your role as your child's advocate:

❖ You will need to put your request in writing and be determined in your goal of getting what your child needs.

- Contact the school or the school district to identify the person to whom your letter should be sent.

- It is important to get the correct spelling of the person's name and the correct title.

❖ If you are unsuccessful in finding out the specific person you need to contact concerning your requests for your child, direct your inquiries or letters to the school principal.

- He or she will ultimately be responsible for ensuring your child's needs are met. Thus, they will be able to get the ball rolling for your child.

❖ Whatever you send to the point of contact, send a copy to your child's teacher so that he or she is aware of what your concerns are and what is being requested.

❖ Keep copies of everything you do concerning your child's education.

The Expected Response

The IDEA stipulates that school administrators must respond to requests related to IEPs or special needs protocols in a 'timely manner' or within a 'reasonable period of time.'

❖ School districts will generally define a 'reasonable period of time' in terms of a certain number of days. You will need to check with your school district to identify what is defined for your child's school.

❖ If not the school, contact the school district's main office for information.

❖ Once you contact the school, wait for the defined period of time.

▪ If you have not heard from the school within the time frame identified, make calls to determine if your letter was received.

▪ If not, resend. If so, be sure you understand the next steps and follow up.

Support for Family Sanity

I encourage you to take advantage of every support resource you have available to you. When my son had the accident that resulted in a Traumatic Brain Injury diagnosis, I was clueless about where to go for help, assistance, or support. Many times, I felt alone and lost on what to do to ensure that my child had as much help as possible to maximally position him to have a successful life.

I was so focused on just doing the best I could, that I did not know how to do any in-depth research on the subject. Had I done so, I would have realized there was a lot of information available on resources and support for parents and families of a child who has special needs; not as much as there is today, but more than I took advantage of at the time. I have included a list of resources at the end of the book to help on your journey, and below are a few suggestions for creating an environment of support for you and your child:

❖ If there are other family members in the household, realize that the special need is not something that just affects the child with the condition. The entire family is impacted, and all should embrace that reality.

❖ Talk to everyone about the special need to include the pros and cons of the condition. Make sure you clearly help each family member understand how the condition impacts the entire family. I made a major mistake in not talking to my son's siblings about their brother's condition and the limitations he would face as time progressed. As a result, I realized, almost too late, that they did not understand the struggles he had to face on a daily basis.

❖ The entire family must be advocates for the special needs of the child. Keep the whole family in the loop when there are medical appointments, IEP meetings, and other special sources of information and instructions.

- Share the research and findings with siblings, grandparents, close family. All should support the child and their needs. This strengthens family.

- Their support and encouragement will lay the foundation for what the child believes he or she can achieve.

❖ Surround yourself with supportive people. Naysayers need to be forbidden and avoided.

- You will have enough to guard against to ensure your child can be the best success story they can be.

- You don't need to have to deal with negative or unsupportive individuals in you or your child's life. Such individuals will make an already difficult journey more difficult.

- Even well-meaning naysayers and negative people should be kept at arm's length.

❖ Don't beat yourself up for feeling frustration and fatigue at times. Being the parent of a child with special needs is a 24-7 job. I had many sleepless nights, and sometimes frustration would set in. Then I would feel guilty for feeling frustrated. It felt like a dizzying merry-go-round of emotions. I had to continuously fall back on prayer, God's grace, and the love of my son to regain my place of peace.

▪ Lean heavily on your faith and God's grace when you feel overwhelmed, fatigued, frustration, irritation, isolation, and the gamut of other emotions that will hit you at one time or another.

▪ Permit yourself to feel what you feel and know it's okay to feel how you feel. When you begin to feel emotionally exhausted or drained, listen to your body and find a way to take time to regroup.

▪ When you get to that place, ask for help. Pull on your support system to try to get a few hours to yourself to relax and exhale.

- This does not mean they have to be blood relatives. I moved from Huntsville, AL, where my support was my ex-husband. When I moved to Atlanta, I knew not one person. Being an ex-military spouse, I mastered the art of building a 'family' out of the friends and church members.

- Get to know the people you connect to. Ask God to connect you to people who you can trust. As I got to know individuals who came into my environment, certain individuals that I found trustworthy became the support system that I needed. Pray first, and God will answer.

- Let go of pride or that erroneous voice in your head that says, 'as a parent, I should be able to handle this.' When you need help, open your

146

mouth, and say so. Generally, God will already have connected you to a source of help if you open your mind to ask for what you need.

- Don't feel guilty for being human. Take care of yourself, so you can be more diligent about taking care of your child.
  - Get the rest you need to keep yourself mentally focused and try not to miss meals. Lack of rest or inadequate nourishment will lead to you being irritable and impatient with your child.
  - Remember, their world revolves around you. You need to be the strongest you that you can be.
- Be consistently mindful of who and what you allow in your physical and emotional space. Not everyone you meet will need to be around you or your child.

❖ Realize that just as you get tired and frustrated, so will your child.
- They will have their times of irritation, anger at their situation, and resentment at their limitations.
- This will be magnified as they get older, and they realize what they can't or may never be able to do. Let your patience and empathy overflow.
- When you notice these emotional struggles in your child, talk to a counselor and ask for guidance on how best to handle what your child is going through.
- You can always start with the school counselor, who should be able to provide recommendations.
- If you are affiliated with a church, talk to your Pastor if you need to. He or she will likely know of other possible resources to tap into.

147

For more strategies for success on your child's educational journey, I recommend a powerful book called *From Emotions to Advocacy* by Peter and Pamela Wright. Standing firmly as your child's advocate and ensuring that you take care of yourself, you can position your child to maximize their potential and be the best they can be.

CHAPTER 9
THE FOSTER PARENT PARADIGM

"The value of Foster Care is immeasurable...because children can never have too many people to love them." Unknown

Each state's family and children services systems do all they can to provide food, clothing, and shelter for every child brought into its care. Part of the charge of a state agency system is to identify structured family environments to help enhance the child's growth as much as possible in dire circumstances. The systems rely on foster care to make that happen. Unfortunately, some foster care situations have failed to promote maximum growth, but instead have made some very young journeys even more difficult.

Children who enter the foster care system are already traumatized by fear, anger, confusion, turmoil, and disruption. Even teens, who think they know what's going on, don't understand the deep-seeded issues that prompt parents to abuse and neglect their own children or allow others to do so. This type of mis-parenting stems from traumas that likely occurred from their own childhood. Thus, it becomes critically important for foster parent to do their best to nurture and water the seed within a traumatized child with encouraging words, caring attitudes, and a posture of a loving parent.

As a foster parent, no matter how long you have charge over caring for the child, you can nurture their seed of promise to help them hang on to the hope for their future. Children who have to experience time in the foster care system often find themselves facing serious educational challenges, which makes it difficult for them to excel in school. Compared to children in mainstream home situations, foster children have lower scores on standardized tests, experience higher school absenteeism, and increased school truancy. Research supports that children in foster care are at greater risk of dropping out of high school, less likely to pursue a college education, and less prone to pursuing dreams and goals. It is imperative that those who take on the mantle of being foster parents to fully understand how critical foster parenting is to the journey of a foster child's journey to success.

Foster Children Educational Challenge

Understanding the unique needs of foster care children related to educational opportunities begins with understanding the foster care system and its challenges related to a stable educational foundation. The Code of Federal Regulations (CFR) Title 45 defines foster care as "24-hour substitute care for children placed away from their parents or guardians."

For various reasons related to child safety, children in foster care may be removed from the homes of their birth parents and placed under state care for what is deemed for their good. With parents working closely with child welfare agencies, some children ultimately can be returned to their birth families. However, many are placed in the long-term foster care system, putting them in situations that makes a strong educational foundation a challenge.

I have experience working in a child welfare agency and know how challenging their efforts are in seeking to do what's best for these at-risk children. The agencies do the best they can to ensure these precious children have food, clothing, shelter, and a safe place to live. However, in that process, a child may be moved many times in a given year. Each move will likely come with moving to a new school. That means the child will have constant disruption in guardian care (foster parents) and school environments.

According to the U.S Department of Health and Human Services, national statistics support the following distressing statistics:

❖ With the more than 600,000 children experiencing foster care in the United States each year, most spend an average of 21.8 months in the system.

❖ 20% will stay in the system for more than three years; 9% remained in the system for five or more years.

❖ 75% of children in foster care generally perform below their grade level in school.

❖ 50% of foster care youth will never graduate from high school or obtain GED.

❖ Only 15% of foster children attend college, and fewer than 3% will earn a college degree.

❖ 65% of adults who were formerly in foster care experienced seven or more school changes between kindergarten and 12th grade.

❖ More than 20,000 youth who age out of foster care do so without experiencing the stability of a 'forever' or permanent family.

❖ Roughly 55% of children in foster care, awaiting adoption, will have multiple placements, and change elementary school numerous times.

Unlike their peers in traditional family structures, children in foster care generally do not have an adequate safety net, social network, nor a solid family structure to ensure the consistency and structure that is the normal path to lay a foundation for educational success. A large body of research consistently suggests that children in foster care are among the most at risk for poor life outcomes in American society.

Adults who are products of the foster care system are documented as more likely than the general population to be homeless, higher unemployment, prone to low-skill jobs, and dependent on welfare or Medicaid. They are also more likely to be convicted of crimes and incarcerated, to succumb to drug and alcohol abuse, or to have poor physical or mental health. Women who have been in foster care experience higher rates of early pregnancy and may be more likely to see their own children placed in foster care. These dire statistics point to a critical need for those who chose to be foster parents to be vigilant and purposeful in how they foster and the care they give to the children placed in their care.

Educational Obstacles Warning Signs

Educational research focused on foster care supports that issues manifest early for many foster children. One study in the state of Washington assessed 4500 public school students in the foster care system and found that children in foster care scored 16 to 20 % below non-foster children on state standardized tests. These results are consistent with national findings.

❖ The National Conference of State Legislatures reported that foster children had "high rates of grade retention, lower scores on standardized tests, and higher absenteeism, tardiness, truancy, and dropout rates" when compared to the general population.

❖ Research from the American School Board Journal surmised that children in foster care are prone to repeat a grade and are twice as likely to drop out of school before graduation when compared to their counterparts.

Understanding these problems and challenges is important for foster parents as they embark on a journey to encourage educational excellence in those in their foster care supervision.

The Foster Parenting Dilemma

Taking on the mantle of foster care parenting is a huge decision because it means taking in a child or children who have suffered some level of trauma. These children may not be classified as special needs as defined by the ADA or the IDEA, but these children in every other way have very targeted specialized needs on their journey. Below are some of the challenges that current foster parents and those considering foster parenting should be aware of as they embrace the difficulties of being foster parents who make a difference.

❖ **Child Placement Instability.**

- Frequent out-of-home placements of youths in foster care invariably leads to frequent school transfers because children can be required to change schools when they change addresses.

- Research suggests that frequent school transfers and disruptions in the learning process can take a toll on a student's learning development, which can result in below grade level performance in reading and math, or lead to the student repeating a grade.

- Frequent changes in placements force children to have to adjust to new classroom settings, teachers, and classmates, which results in loss of social networks, peer groups, and relationships. These frequent disruptions in stability and home changes escalate emotional insecurity and anxiety in children in the system. These frequent moves also escalate fears, anxiety, and worry which often is exhibited in negative and difficult behaviors.

- Foster parents will need to be prepared to deal with the hurt, disappointment, frustration, and anger that these precious and confused children will likely display.

❖ **Persistent Low Expectations of Youth.**

- Surveys of adults who were formerly in foster care found that many were very displeased with their educational experiences. They felt that the foster care system failed to encourage high expectations for their education.

- One survey found that older youth in foster care reported having high aspirations of what they wanted for their lives; however, they felt that those they encountered did not support their lead. As a result of the lack of support of their goals, they felt resentment and anger that others had low expectations of them and their education. In essence, they felt that those charged with their care actually undermined their capacity to achieve success in educational pursuits.

- These former foster care individuals consistently responded that they would have benefited from adults who encouraged them to excel.

- Foster parents must understand the expectations of their foster care charges. Most have desires and dreams; they are just afraid to allow themselves to dream too much for fear of living further disappointments.

154

- The greatest thing a foster parent can do is let their foster child know that they have the potential to be anyone they desire if they just don't give up.

- One ex-foster child told her story that highlights the power of one foster parent's impact in a short period of time. She was in and out of foster care homes as long as she could remember, some good, some not at all good. She stated that she would intentionally not get too comfortable or attached to any family with whom she was placed because she knew she would have to leave sooner or later. She explained that some tried to include her in the family; some did not, and none ever talked to her about her future, so she never really thought about her tomorrow.

  However, she said one foster parent with whom she only spent a few weeks told her that she had great potential; they could see it. They told her that she should not allow her current situation to keep her from working hard to be who she wanted to be and to hold on to her dreams. She said for the entire few weeks she was with them, they encouraged her to dream big. When she told her story, she was preparing to graduate college with honors! The positive and inspiring words of one foster parent who only had her for a few weeks help her believe that she was more than her circumstances.

- Foster parents must take every moment you have with a foster child placed in your care to speak life into them and encourage them to dream bigger than the limitations they are living. You never know how just one word from you can revive a lost dream and inspire greatness.

❖ **Special Education Impact.**

- The delivery of special education services is another area of potential difficulty for children in foster care. One study found that as many as 30 – 40% of all children in foster care are also in special education, a percentage that is well above the average for the general population.

- The nature of the special education system suggests that many foster children are being poorly served. Special needs children require strong parental advocacy, which requires a high and consistent level of dedication to ensuring that the child receives the critically needed services required for success.

- Children who experience multiple placements and corresponding school transfers may experience gaps in the delivery of needed special education services. Additionally, the consistency of parental/guardian intervention as well as changing IEP team member makes a strong foundation of continuity of care an almost impossibility. As a result, special needs children in the foster care system often are not well served to aid in maximizing their potential.

- Foster parents who take a child in their home should ensure they clearly understand any special needs of the child in their care. If there is an IEP special need, foster parents must be committed to getting that child as much in services as they can while the child is in their care. It may only be for a short period of time, but anything or any time that can enhance a child's potential for success is not wasted time.

❖ Foster Parent Interventions

To succeed in educational pursuits, a child in foster care needs his or her foster parents to be engaged, invested, and involved.

- The decision to take a child in a difficult situation into the home mandates someone with a big heart, a generous spirit, and a willingness to invest the time needed to address the unique needs of the child they embrace.

- Foster parents must be willing to lead the charge to fight for the child they decide to take into their care, with the understanding that it's about investing in the child, not about how much time the child may or may not be in the home.

- These children cannot be seen as extra income or extra help in the home. Such thought processes or self-interested strategies is the reason the dismal statistics exist related to what these precious children believe they are worth. If you take on the mantle of foster parenting, do it for the right reason, and treat these children with the love and care that every child deserves.

- These precious ones must be treated as members of the family and integrated in the home and the family dynamic. If this is not the case, they will know that they are just a temporary meal ticket and respond accordingly. Remember, it only takes one foster parent to impart the right word into the broken spirit of a foster child to revive hope in that child.

- As a foster parent, introduce them as *your child*, not *your foster child*. This very minor shift in the introduction is significant to the child and will be vital to helping them feel more integrated into the family dynamic. A dear friend of mine was a foster care parent with two boys of her own. She says that when she fostered, she never introduced her foster children as foster children. They were just 'her children.' Every expectation she had of her birth sons, she instilled in her foster sons. What she did for her birth sons, she did for her foster sons. To this day, they remember her and the love she showed them.

- If you are a person of faith, the most powerful thing you can do for your foster child as a foster parent is to pray for their strength, safety, and perseverance. No matter how long or short their stay with you, pray over them daily. Prayers are like seeds that are planted. Some produce quickly. Some germinate for a while. Every prayer you pray over your foster child will reap a harvest in due season. Those prayers will not be wasted.

These precious children did not ask for the situations in which they found themselves. The circumstances that resulted in their placement in the foster care system are not situations that were in their control. They are only children who still desire and need love, acceptance, support, and EVERY opportunity to be the best they can be. So, even if it is only for a little while, each moment a foster parent has with a child in the foster care system must be a moment to motivate, inspire, and pour the best the foster parent has into that child.

Foster Parent Engagement

If each foster parent that touches the life of a foster child does not fight for the child, that child will be set up to fail and will have a difficult path to any potential for success. The key to laying a strong foundation for the time the child is in your care is to set reasonable and realistic expectations for the child with the clear message that you believe in them and their potential despite the difficulty of their circumstances. Make no mistake about it; it won't always be easy.

Don'ts of the Foster Parent Connections:

❖ Do not make the child's already traumatized journey worse by inflicting more pain with neglect, hurtful words, or dismissive attitudes that tell the child they don't matter.

❖ Do not engage in foster parenting just for the monthly stipend. Your role in the brief time you have with the child is so much greater than money. One encouraging word from you could change a life.

❖ Do not strip that child of whatever hope and dignity they have left by inflicting the degradation of rape, molestation, or child abuse. They have already suffered enough!

Do's of Foster Parenting:

When you take that child into your home, you are also taking in their hurt, disappointments, fears, apprehensions, and anger. So, what strategies can you, as a foster parent, implement and practice to help lay a foundation for success for each child you touch?

❖ **Do** create open lines of communication with teachers and counselors.

▪ As soon as you know that a child will join your family, reach out to school staff to lay the foundation for a collaborative, positive working relationship. Let teachers, counselors, and administrators know who you are and that they should call or email you with any issues or concerns.

- Focus more on the impact you can make on your foster child's life during that length of time they will be with you. Request regular updates from the child's teachers to stay abreast of how they are doing. Every interaction, every word, every action has the potential of changing that child's life for the good.

❖ **Do** ensure a 2-way avenue of communication.

- Not only should you, as a foster parent, ask the teachers and school administrators to let you know if something is not going as expected, or otherwise seem amiss; but you should likewise let your child's teachers and administrators know if you notice emotional, behavioral, or academic changes in the child's responses.

- If your foster child is having particular difficulties, inform key school personnel, and seek to work together to address the best next steps.

❖ **Do** seek to make mandatory 'visitation' as minimally disruptive as possible.

- The foster care system includes numerous mandatory, and often emotionally challenging, activities that children in mainstream homes never have to encounter. Visitations are among the most emotionally difficult of those activities.

- Foster children must deal with visits by case managers in the foster care home; visits with the birth parents, which can be an emotional roller coaster for the child; and visitations with school personnel. These visitations alone can manifest embarrassment, anger, and

160

frustration, which can lead to 'acting out.'

- When foster children are having a difficult time with visitations, or are suffering anxiety related to them, foster parents should maintain open lines of communication with the child's teacher.

- Other than you, as the foster parent, the teacher is the one other consistent presence in the child's otherwise disrupted world.

- Never cease to work collaboratively with the school for the good of the child. They may have to deal with going to several different schools in their educational journey, but you can help make the school encounter for that child while in your care a positively impacting one.

- Work collaboratively with the child's case manager to schedule visitation to be as minimally disruptive to the child's day as possible. Remember, they already feel they are 'different.' You are the only advocate that can help them 'feel' as comfortable as possible while they are in your care.

❖ **Do** take a hands-on approach to homework and studying.

- Just because the child may only be assigned to be in your care for a short period of time, as their parent figure for that period, you owe it to them to be their advocate and encourager.

- The one thing that angered adults who were previous foster children was the feeling that those who fostered them did not really care about them, and that they had no expectations of excellence from them. They did not feel that anyone cared about their success. They only wanted the money and provided bare-bones necessities: food, clothing, and shelter. Just keeping a roof over a child's head, providing food and clothing is not enough to meet the needs of a child. They need to be cared for, loved, and encouraged. That's what so many foster children miss on their growth journey.

- Take some time to sit down with the child to talk to them about school, learning, and the expectations of school focus in the home. Be realistic, but let them know early that you believe in their potential. We all need to be encouraged. Your words of encouragement may well be the first time they received such words.

- Make time to sit with the child's teacher about where they are in the learning process, are they on level, what are the challenges, are they in need of special accommodations. Find out where the child's learning ability and level of knowledge is. In collaboration with the teacher, counselor, and the child, work with them where they are.

❖ **Do** attend school functions and volunteer consistently.

- As a foster parent, one of the best things you can do to encourage them to embrace education and learning is to encourage the child to participate in activities outside of the classroom. That means you will also need to be willing to be a bit more active in school interactions.

- Engage your foster child to participate as much as possible, but give them a voice to say 'no' in the situation if they choose. Find out what extracurricular activities the school offers, sit down with the child to discuss what interests them, and make a joint decision on participation.

162

- Even if time with you is limited, embrace the reality that during that period, however brief, the foster child is YOUR child.

❖ **Do** impart positive seeds in the child.

- It is important to remember that many social or positive interpersonal skills were likely not taught, nor valued, in your child's previous home. Otherwise, they would not likely be in the foster care system. So, realistically, skills that you may take for granted are absent and will take time to develop. The best way to teach such skills is to let your foster child see the positive seed in action…kindness, warmth, compassion, etc.

- Encourage your child to spread his or her wings and to try new experiences. Show them the experience of giving back to the community. Your volunteer time investment in volunteer endeavors does not need to be extensive. Volunteer as long or as little as you like; and let them join you. Show them that caring for other is not only rewarding, but fun. That lesson alone can deposit so much in their broken spirit.

- A good place to volunteer is the child's school. Studies support that children, in any situation, who have parents volunteer in school activities, generally have better grades, score higher on tests, and have better social skills and behavior. All children need to see this paradigm in action; foster children are in greater need of seeing this level of participation. It tells them that despite their circumstances, they matter!

Foster Parent Challenges and Cautions

❖ **Do not** assume caseworkers will pass along all the needed information. Your child's caseworker has a lot on his or

163

her plate. Unfortunately, many are often overworked, underpaid, and sometimes overwhelmed. They do great work with the resources and time they have.

- Expect them to share all that is needed with you, but be aware that sometimes some tidbits may get omitted. It's often just the nature of the massive amount of work these workers have on their plate.

- Some tasks may not be shared or completed with the immediacy that you might prefer, such as the child may not be placed in a new school immediately, transcripts may not get to the school timely, the child may have to miss a few days before official enrollment.

- These challenges can cause residual lash back and problems with the child's transition to his or her new school environment as well as acclimation to your home.

- You will want to have a strategic conversation with the caseworker to find out some timelines and stay on top of the processes.

❖ **Do not** assume schools will automatically have resources and information needed to meet the child's needs.

- The reality of the situation is that it is very difficult in today's educational climate for teachers to be experts at dealing with the unique situations that so many children are subject to. As with so many areas of life, the unique needs of children in foster care are often overlooked.

- Teachers are not trained in the foster care system. They have so many other paradigms to deal with in the classroom, and they generally don't have the capacity to be consistently mindful of the foster care child's unique needs.

- While foster parents undergo rigorous and extensive training before taking a child into their homes, teachers and educators do not have any specialized foster care training. As a result, as the parent, you will have to wear the mantle of being your child's advocate.

- You will need to have apt communication with your child's teachers and counselors to assure a plan of action to lay a strong foundation to maximize the child's educational potential. Get to know your child and pass your knowledge on to the school.

❖ **Do not** expect your foster child to have strong academic performances in a new school.

- In general, foster children tend to perform below level in regard to both academic performance and positive behavior as compared to their counterparts. Statistically, most children in foster care are behind in math and reading skills, which are two of the most critical fundamental skill areas related to academic success.

- Many foster children are behind in academic knowledge; have poor, sometimes failing, scores; and are often held back from being promoted to the next grade level. The longer the child is in the system, the more likely these statistical paradigms will prevail. The sad fact is research supports that 55% of youth in foster care will drop out of school before high school graduation.

- It is imperative that as a foster parent, you understand the educational challenges you will have to face with your child. By understanding the challenges, you can better position to work with your child, the teacher, the case manager, the school counselor, and other key professionals who can help you help your child be victorious over these challenges.

❖ **Do not** assume your foster child will be excited about attending a new school. They generally won't be.

- Foster children have a difficult time acclimating to the 'new' paradigms in their lives – new parents, new home, new school, new surroundings. They are only children and don't have the capacity to be logical, reasonable, rational, or any other concepts that they are often expected to exhibit. Children as a rule seek stability.

- The foster care system at its very core is unstable. As such, foster youth will not be happy with the massive change of the new environment. They don't have the mental capacity to react to the level of massive change with positivity. The brain functioning of school-age children is still extremely emotional. As a result, that's how they respond to situations, including reactions to a new school environment.

- Often times, school is a constant reminder that they are foster children without a real home, different from the rest of the kids. As an adult, we find it difficult to be seen as and treated differently, even if it is only our perception. Needless to say, for a child, this is an extremely difficult place to be, and a hard situation to deal with. The continuous reminder that their peers are living with biological family members, while they are not, is a difficult reality for them.

- You may see, hear, and experience them acting out in different ways. Some children simply withdraw and become antisocial in an attempt to escape their current environment; others might react with violent behavior,

166

disrupting the classroom and the home. This, unfortunately, is the reason many children are moved so often in the system, resulting in another 'new' home and another 'new' school.

As the parent and advocate of your foster child, you will have to be patient, kind, understanding, and constantly forgiving in order to help your child get past the broken stage on the road to becoming whole. Your capacity to embrace them even in their anger, hurt and brokenness can be the key to helping them let their walls down so you can engage and get them to a place of healing and wholeness.

Personal Education Plan (PEP)

As an advocate, you will often need to be definitive in working with your case manager on matters related to how to manage various aspects of your foster child's care and education. That's where the Personal Education Plan (PEP) comes in.
The PEP, also known as the Care Plan, outlines the child's needs and specifies and documents the services required to meet those needs. It is a record of what needs to happen for the child to enable them to fulfill their potential and reflects education plans, special educational needs, and plans to address unique situations related to the child's foster care placement.

The PEP outlines the goals for the child, strategies to achieve goals and short and long term desired outcomes. Often, the agency in whose care that child is placed will have a PEP in place when the child comes to you. It's important that you sit down to thoroughly review what has been outlined when the child enters your home, so you will know the child's history and projected plans.

As you review the PEP, several components should be included. Although educational goals are a critical part of the plan, the document should also focus on the following:

* Social interactions, challenges, and goals.

* Personal development.

* Religious and cultural identity.

* Assessment of personal strengths and areas of concern.

* Opportunities to develop interests, skills, and personal 'character'.

* Educational experiences and opportunities.

* Support through transition points.

As you work with your child and learn more about the child, do not hesitate to contact the case manager if you feel some component of the PEP needs to be redressed. Some agency systems will change or update the PEP without coordinating or collaborating with the foster parents. Your goal is always to have a collaborative relationship with your child's case management team, but do ensure that you are included in the plans for the child's future and educational endeavors. As you get to know and understand your child, be forthright in contacting your child's case manager about potentially updating the PEP as needed.

Position for Foster Care Success

Remember, as you embark on the foster parenting journey, you are the child's parent and primary advocate, even if the time is for a short period. Do everything that any good parent would do to promote their child's educational aspirations and support their achievements. Realize that you will need to master the art of communication to maximize communication with your child's caseworker, teachers, counselors, and other professionals related to your child's care and well-being. You will need to be supremely patient as you help them get past the anger, distrust, and fear of a new paradigm.

Becoming a foster parent is not for the faint of heart. Even if the governing family service agency tells you that the child will only by in your care for a short period of time, you must be strong enough and focused enough to ensure that you make the most of each moment you have with that child. If and when you decide to take the foster parenting journey, you will need to walk a fine line between being 100% emotionally invested in the child, while understanding that outcomes may not always be what you desire.

Seek God's guidance every step of the way, from your decision to be a foster parent, to seeking to understand the unique needs of the child, to your interaction to help position the child for success. You will need to pour into them when so much has been taken from them at such an early age. You will need to saturate them with hope, love, and inspiration. Treat them as if your interaction with them will be the only positive light they will ever see. Show them the true AGAPE style of love that God shows us. Love that is non-judgmental and unconditional. All you do and every decision you make concerning your foster charge must be with one goal in mind: doing what's best for the child.

If you feel that you have the spiritual strength, tenacity, resilience, emotional intelligence, and the positive mental energy to invest in embracing a child in the foster care system, there is a child waiting for you to connect. Just think... the love you pour into a foster child and the hope you inspire could be the key to them prevailing past their detrimental circumstances to excel in education and life. What a phenomenal legacy!

Chapter 10
Destiny Detractors – In Home

The strongest people aren't those who win medals, but the people who refuse to give up when they face trials and difficulties."
Ashley Hodgeson

Laying a strong foundation for your child to succeed in school during their formative years mandates a fundamental knowledge of issues and paradigms that can undermine a child's focus and capacity to achieve educational goals. As the primary advocate for your child, you, as a parent, must be conscientious of threats to your child's capacity to reach their full capacity and achieve all that God meant for them to be. Parents and primary guardians must understand that they are responsible for assuring that youth are positioned for success in all they do in school and life.

Childhood should be a time of growth and positive development in caring families and supportive communities. However, many children find themselves facing issues that impact their development negatively, and that undermines their capacity to be the best they can be. A critical aspect of laying a strong positive development foundation is ensuring that "Destiny Detractors" don't derail the potential they possess. Destiny Detractors are any external issue that detract from or undermine a child's capacity to succeed. Detrimental impact research supports that several critical paradigms can serve to critically undermine a child's capacity to be successful in school, or in having the motivation to pursue success long term. Two of the factors that affect children in the home include childhood poverty and childhood molestation.

Childhood Poverty Distress

Children's physical health and brain development depend on them being well-fed, particularly in the earliest years of life. Hunger and malnutrition jeopardize children's health, development, education, and career readiness. Research since 2015 consistently supports that nearly 1 in 5 children in America live in homes that lack enough food to ensure appropriate nourishment to ensure appropriate physical and mental growth. Research further supports that more than 3 million children in the United States are living in homes at a poverty level that is equal to some of the poorest countries in the world. This results in many children going to school every day without breakfast and going to sleep at night on hungry stomachs.

Currently, fifty-one percent of pre-K through 12th-grade students reside in low-income households with 31% of that number being single mother households. Children who grow up in poverty will complete fewer years of formal education and will earn a much lower income than children who grow up in households with income above the poverty level. Additionally, children who grow up in poverty are more likely to suffer poor health, which also undermines the capacity to be successful in school. Statistics support that 30% of children raised in poverty laden households do not finish high school. This leads to a cycle of continual poverty since individuals who don't earn a high school diploma by age 20 are seven times more likely to also live in poverty.

Poverty Impact on Education

Despite being one of the most developed countries in the world, the U.S. has one of the highest rates of childhood poverty in the world. Children raised in poverty face several disadvantages, which becomes very evident in the educational process. Some of these youth often suffer the chronic stress of living in complicated, disadvantaged environments that affect brain functioning related to attention span, memory, and ability to reason. They also tend to have more emotional and behavioral problems, which makes the transition to school and structured learning problematic.

Youth in poverty-stricken households face challenges with their cognitive (reasoning) and literary (learning) ability and generally begin school academically and socioeconomically behind their peers from higher-income backgrounds. This impacts a child's overall health and motor skills; diminishes the ability to concentrate and remember information; and reduces attentiveness, focus, and motivation. These dynamics result in children of poverty starting school with what's been termed 'a readiness gap,' which means when they start school their cognitive and mental capacity is not where other children might be, and this gap only grows wider as they grow older.

As a result of the readiness gap, children feel alienated in the school environment; suffer insecurities due to their socioeconomic status; endure feelings of powerlessness and inferiority compared to their fellow students, and grows with some level of at their circumstances. One factor that doctors now notes as it relates to school success is the number of words children hear during their formative years that impact the readiness gap. Research supports that low-income children hear 30 million fewer words by the age of five than their counterparts. This directly impacts how readily they can learn when they enter school, how likely they are to read in their spare time, and will generally result in them having trouble reading altogether.

173

Youth from low-income families are more likely to have lower test scores than their counterparts and are at higher risk of becoming high school dropouts. If they are fortunate enough to complete high school, they are less likely to attend college, which minimizes the likelihood of professional, higher-paying careers. This directly impacts the potential to break the cycle of generational poverty and reduce the chances of these youth being positioned to lead rewarding, productive lives.

Another driving factor that directly influences a child in poverty is stress. Stress from a child's home environment, poor nutrition, and other factors in a child's life affects a child's physical and cognitive development. The 'stress effect' in a child increases the likelihood of developmental delays, learning problems, and behavioral issues in children. As they grow, they are more at risk of experiencing depression, drug abuse, diabetes, alcoholism, and other health problems in adulthood.

This impacts a youth's motivation, capacity, and desire to do well in school. Research supports that a poverty-environment promotes the part of the child's brain that regulates emotion and behavior (the limbic system) to send constant messages of fear and stress to the prefrontal cortex, which controls motivation, memory, problem-solving, and goal setting. These negative developmental aspects positions children in poverty situations to be six times more likely to drop out of high school and not obtain a diploma. The downward domino effect will generally result in these dropouts being more likely to end up on public assistance, engage in criminal activity, and suffer other negative societal misfortunes.

With more than 50 percent of school-aged children now coming from low-income families, the educational process for them is already a risky journey. Although this may seem like a dismal picture, all is definitely not lost. There are several things parents and guardians can do to counter the potential negative influences of a low-income environment. Despite the difficulties financial constraints can place on the family dynamic, a child can achieve great success when they are taught to be determined, persistent, resilient, optimistic, and self-controlled.

The Parents Supportive Guidance

The most important focus of a parent in laying a strong foundation for educational success is to ensure an environment conducive to learning, positive growth, self-esteem, and success. Research supports that the first thing a child needs is loving, safe, consistent support and positive attention. Homes that are rife with abuse (of any kind), domestic violence, drug or alcohol addiction, or mental health problems makes that kind of support null and void.

They don't get what they need for positive development, and they will suffer the consequences, personally and academically. Research also reveals that children in lower-income homes get twice as many reprimands or negative feedback as positive comments, whereas middle-class homes provide three positive comments to one negative comment.

As a result of these occurrences, students of low-income families are at higher risk of lower educational performance, to include higher dropout rates. Signs of students at risk of dropping out of school include the following:

❖ High rate of absenteeism, frequent tardiness, or truancy.

❖ Limited participation in extracurricular activities.

175

❖ Exhibiting feelings of isolation or exclusion; not belonging.

❖ Not identifying with the school 'family' or fitting with the school's culture.

❖ Continual poor grades, including failing in subjects or failing grade levels.

❖ Consistent low scores in reading or mathematics, which lead to feelings of failure.

❖ Acting out in negative ways; exhibiting disinterest in academic success.

Parents, as a child's first teacher, is critical to laying the right foundation for success. In addition to the strategies already discussed in this book, below are the fundamental strategies that a caring parent must be mindful to ensure that their child will be a success in school despite humble beginnings:

❖ Have a frank talk with your child about the importance of being proud of who they are, and not base their sense of self on what they have or how they dress.

❖ Talk to your child about the value of self-worth, emphasizing that no matter what, you love, support, and value them above all else. Saturate them with your love and support.

❖ Regularly talk with your child about his or her school day, ensuring that you are present to hear what they are saying verbally and non-verbally.

❖ Encourage your child to read at home. Help them expand their horizons by reading about things outside of just what they experience. This will help expand their vision of possibilities.

❖ Be a role model in encouraging your child to read. If your child is young, start now. Show them that reading is fundamental and in the process, encourage them to dream big. Many parents discourage big dreams for fear of setting a child up for disappointment. Remember, life is not living without the hope to dream.

❖ Talk to your child's teachers and school counselor about what you see at home and to obtain updates on grades and behavior in school. When needed, ask for help in identifying resources available to help your child with any noted areas of concern.

❖ Watch who your child hangs out with, which means you really, *really* need to monitor social media and phone calls. Ensure that they are involved in healthy activities, which may mean that your home may need to be the place they 'hang out', so you can monitor.

❖ Be vigilant about knowing what is going on in your community and your school. Since finances will likely not allow you to connect your child to programs with a cost associated, you need to target free programs. Work with your school and organizations to get your child involved in activities to give them opportunities to grow and shine. Boys and Girls Clubs, Boy Scouts, Girl Scouts, Big Brothers & Big Sisters are just a few to check out.

❖ Expose your child to things outside of your immediate environment. Find out what is going on in your community, your town, and surrounding areas that you and your family can participate in for free. Take a drive through a neighborhood that is outside of the poverty zone. Show them there is more to this big world than just what they see and experience every day. Give them a foundation to dream and hope for more.

❖ Resist *negative parenting*, which is the propensity to react to negative situations or stressful situations with emotionalism. This can be yelling, screaming, profanity, blaming (especially the child). This can, and generally will affect your child's ability to regulate his or her own emotion, because they learn behaviors from their #1 influence…the parent. This learned negative responsiveness will create ongoing problems in a child's interpersonal interactions and learning engagement. Parents who can help their child handle stress or the unexpected with calm focus teaches a child to think through issues and deal with conflict positively.

❖ Be a role-model of emotional resilience. When you experience drama or trauma situations that causes anger, disappointment, frustration, hurt, sadness, or other negative emotional reactions, it is important that you child observe your calm positive reaction. This is the foundation of teaching your child how to handle negativity with grace and maturity. Teach them how to handle difficulties without freaking out, stressing out, or giving up.

❖ Ensure a safe place for your child to land. Your home cannot be a place a child fears. Unfortunately, sometimes the financial hardships of poverty bring out the negative sides of personalities, and often children suffer the brunt of that frustration, i.e., child abuse, yelling, hurtful words, neglect.

❖ No matter the situation, you are the only defense your child has to help them be and feel safe. Your stress will become their stress. Whatever you have to do, ensure they have a safe place to come home to at all cost. If you need help, don't fear to reach out to get the help you need. Your child and his or her future depends on it.

The Educator's Encouragement

A big drawback for low-income students is the interactions they experience in the school environment. Sometimes, some educators don't have time to invest in helping children who present challenges in the classroom. Unfortunately, low-income youth may present challenges that teachers may find more of a distraction to teaching the rest of the class. As a result, these youth may be labeled attitudinal, unmotivated, difficult.

Students from low-income homes are more likely to struggle with classroom engagement and will appear to be purposefully difficult. These attitudes could be the result of fear of rejection, anxiety about how they are perceived, worry about home situations, anger about the home situation, embarrassment about their low-income state, etc. Although dealing with students in poverty situation is uncomfortable, the reality is that it is a real paradigm that teachers must deal with.

Many don't want to accept that different strategies are needed to get through to these youth who are most negatively impacted. However, research across the spectrum clearly tells us that poverty and low-income students struggle with classroom engagement and educational success. If teachers and parents don't take purposeful action to counter some effects, students with great potential may get lost in the maze. The following scenarios summarizes the challenges of classroom engagement:

❖ Children of low-income households are less likely to eat healthy breakfast, get proper exercise, get proper diagnoses for conditions that might impact learning, receive appropriate medical attention, or be prescribed appropriate medications or interventions. All these adversely affect cognition, learning, and attendance.

❖ Children who grow up in poverty conditions typically have smaller vocabularies than their counterparts. This increases the likelihood of academic failure.

❖ Children of low-income households can come across as unmotivated. This is generally because financial hardships can result in depressive symptoms, which manifest in a lack of hope, feelings of helplessness, and low optimism about the future.

❖ Children in low-income homes exhibit cognitive problems resulting in short attention spans, being easily distracted, difficulty monitoring the quality of their work, and difficulty in problem-solving.

❖ Disruptive home relationships, such as domestic violence or child abuse, often results in students having a basic distrust of adults. If adults have failed them at home, children may believe that the adults in school will fail them as well. Acting out in the classroom can often be an extension of that mistrust.

❖ The stressors at home can cause children to be stressed out. Distressed children will generally exhibit one of two behaviors: angry, irate assertiveness or disconnected passivity ('leave me alone'). Neither of these behaviors supports the child's potential or capacity to learn. It's a defense mechanism that will take some time and effort to get through to them.

So, what can teachers do to help the child succeed? Below are some actions that teachers can take to help:

❖ Get to know the parents of the children you are entrusted with educating. A few phone calls will tell you much of what you need to know about how you will need to interact with your students.

❖ In a teacher's strategy, a good course of action is to infuse vocabulary building exercises in the classroom instruction strategy. This will help students with issues in this area expand their vocabulary without calling low-income students out in front of their peers.

❖ Don't make quick assumptions that a child is 'lazy' or 'unmotivated' without digging deeper. Engage to strengthen your relationship with your students to get to know them as individuals. This will also help those from low-income homes build a foundation of trust in you as a teacher. Show them you care. Depending upon the situation, you may be the only one who believes in them.

❖ As a teacher, make an effort to connect to the student in ways to help them see the classroom as a place of hope. Help them see learning as more than just something to do because someone says they must. Tie the classroom lesson to their real world. Make learning relevant and help them see how learning can help them make dreams a reality.

❖ Infuse your teaching strategy with words of affirmation. Affirm every student's effort in every achievement in class. Research tells us that when teachers give more positives than negatives, student learning is optimized. Just one positive word can have a powerful impact on a child who rarely hears it at home.

❖ Rather than put a label on students in disadvantaged situations, hold them accountable for being more than they think they can be. Let them know you believe that they can do or be more; then hold them accountable for doing and being more. Affirm and reinforce their efforts when they achieve, helping them build a foundation of self-value.

❖ Children from disadvantaged, stress-filled homes are particularly in need of positive, encouraging, caring adults. Teachers have a strong influence in these situations. Take time to get to know names, hobbies, interests, and family dynamics. Your interest may well be the catalyst to help them see a bright future rather than one that is bleak.

❖ As a teacher, help students embrace coping skills so they can better deal with their stressors (family and school). When behaviors surface that are unacceptable, hold them accountable; let them know in a caring, yet firm voice what is and is not allowed.

❖ Remember, a teacher who establishes a foundation of mutual respect, caring concern, and support can provide a student with the necessary skills needed to thrive in and out of school. One teacher can change a child's life.

Remember, students in poverty or disadvantaged environments are not broken or damaged. They just have challenges to face, all of which can be overcome with the right investment of time and focus. A child's brain is highly adaptable and can embrace new experiences quickly. They just need to know someone believes in them. Be that someone.

Protection from Predators

No parent likes to think of their child being hurt or victimized. Everyone likes to think of the bad things that happen are things that happen to other people. The thought is if they don't dwell on it, they like to think it just won't happen to them. Statistics about our youth and what they go through in today's society do not support 'the blind eye' mentality as feasible. Parents must be on duty 24/7. They don't have the luxury of taking a vacation from parenting. Parents must be cognizant of what's going on with their child, who is influencing their child, and know the nuances of their child when the child has human interactions. As a parent, you just can't listen to what your child says with their words. You must listen to their non-verbals more than you do their verbals.

Let's first clarify the definition of terms used in connection with child sexual abuse. There is confusion regarding the terms, 'child molester' and 'pedophile.' For those who take time to think about it, the terms have become synonymous with the term pedophile just a fancy word for a child molester. There is no single or uniform definition for the word pedophile. Mental-health professionals identify it as a psychiatric diagnosis with specific criteria. We won't get into the specifics of how mental health professionals define pedophiles, but we do want to give a foundational clarity to the definitions.

Not all pedophiles are child molesters. A child molester is an individual who actually engages in sexual acts with a child. A pedophile is one who has a preference for children as sexual objects and fantasize about having sex with them; however, if they do not act on that preference or those fantasy with a child, he is not a child molester. A person cannot be arrested for being a pedophile if he or she has not acted on the desire. Once the preference has been acted upon, the individual can (and should) be arrested for child molestation. This is when they become known as child predators. As a parent, you should be vigilant about both individuals. If you have any suspicions about how someone looks at, pays attention to, or interacts with your child, better be safe than sorry. Don't leave them alone with your child.

The Statistics Speak

A child being abused is a parent's worst nightmare. When faced with the reality, the parent will generally feel anger, fury, and outrage. Additionally, comes the guilt and recriminations that they failed to keep their child safe. Many parents, in their hopes and belief that 'this could never happen' in their family, choose to not talk about it in the home, especially with their children. Parents also often avoid the conversation of sex, which makes the topic somewhat taboo in the mind of the child. However, failing to have these discussions is one of the worse things the prudent parent can do.

Children need to have conversations about sex and the concepts of sexual abuse at an early age, that is age-appropriate. Removing the stigma of these being taboo topics will help the child understand that you are available of they have questions or concerns. If you are not available to them, they will suffer in silence. The time to start talking to your child about sex is three years old. Remember, the discussions should be age-appropriate, so the conversation won't need to be graphic or detailed.

At this stage, you should not begin to talk about sex right away. You work up to it by starting to talk to them about their

184

body parts as well as good touch/bad touch. Why is it so important for parents to begin to open the door to these types of discussions so early? Abusers can be family members, friends, neighbors, or close family acquaintances. It is imperative that these conversations take place early; and equally critical for parents to watch who is allowed around your babies who can't speak their fears.

Child molesters target children of all ages; so, the ownness is on parents to be constantly conscientious of who they allow around their children and who they entrust to care for their children. Children get abused in places that should be their safe zone or that parents often consider safe places to leave them. These atrocities can occur in the home, at school, church, recreation centers, youth sports leagues, and any other place children gather. Unfortunately, abusers can also be older children that are asked to care for younger ones.

Let's talk about the statistics of how children suffer when they can't talk to their parents.

❖ Of the babies born each year in the U.S., approximately 400,000 will become victims of sexual abuse.

❖ 1 in 7 girls and 1 in 25 boys will be sexually abused before the age of 18.

❖ 90% of children who are victims of abuse know their abuser. Only 10% of sexually abused children are abused by a stranger.

❖ 30% of children who are sexually abused are abused by family members.

❖ As many as 40% of children who are sexually abused are abused by older or more powerful children.

185

❖ The younger the child victim, the more likely it is that the perpetrator is a juvenile. Juveniles are the offenders in 43% of assaults on children under age six. Of these offenders, 14% are under age 12.

❖ The younger the victim, the more likely it is that the abuser is a family member. Of those molesting a child under six, 50% were family members. Family members also accounted for 23% of those abusing children ages 12 to 17.

❖ 60% of abused victims never tell anyone. They suffer in silence.

❖ Although the numbers of reported abuse are declining, the public is not fully aware of the magnitude of the problem.

❖ Only about 38% of child sexual abuse victims disclose the fact they have been sexually abused. Many never disclose while they are going through the abuse.

❖ Most people think of adult rape as a crime of great proportion and significance. However, children are sexually assaulted at a much higher rate than adults.

❖ 70% of all reported sexual assaults (including assaults on adults) occur to children aged 17 and under.

The Child Paradigm Risk Factors

While no child is sheltered from the risk of abuse, some situations significantly increase or reduce the risk of sexual abuse. The following risk factors are based on reported and identified cases of abuse:

❖ Family structure is the most significant risk factor in child sexual abuse.

  ▪ Children who live with two married biological parents are at a low risk for abuse.

186

- The risk increases when children live with stepparents or a single parent.

❖ Children living without either parent (foster children) are ten times more likely to be sexually abused than children that live with both biological parents.

❖ Children who live with a single parent that has a live-in partner are at the highest risk.

- These children are 20 times more likely to be victims of sexual abuse than children living with both biological parents.

❖ Gender is also a critical factor in sexual abuse. Females are five times more likely to be abused than males.

❖ Age is a significant factor in sexual abuse.

- Children are most vulnerable to abuse between the ages of 7 and 13.
- The median age for reported abuse is nine years old.
- However, of children who are abused, more than 20% are abused before the age of 8.

❖ Male victimology has been more reported recently than in the past.

- 8% of victims aged 12-17 are male.
- 26% of victims under the age of 12 are male.

❖ Race and ethnicity are also significant in reported abuse.

- African American children have almost twice the risk of sexual abuse than white children.
- Children of Hispanic ethnicity have a slightly greater risk than non-Hispanic white children.

The Child Molester Strategy

Child molesters follow a common strategy to approach the children that they are interested in. They literally prowl like animal predators to obtain the object of their interest. Scientists have determined that there is a strategy for the way your child might be targeted. It's called the Child Molester 4-Stage Strategy. As a parent, you must understand how they can potentially target and get to your child.

❖ Stage 1: Win the Child's Trust.

- This involves discerning what the child needs and giving it to him or her.

- For instance, if the child is hungry, a molester would offer food. If the child wants a toy, a molester will buy it. If the child needs a father figure, a molester will provide nurturing and guidance.

❖ Stage 2: Create Opportunity.

- This is when the molester monitors family schedules and parental interactions to maneuver times to be with the child when no one else is around to determine when to take the next steps.

❖ Stage 3: Get the Child Alone.

- This is when the molester has scoped out the family situation to get the child alone to abuse him or her. By this time, they have obtained the child's trust.

❖ Stage 4: The Threat Strategy.

- This is what happens after they have attacked the child. They will use tactics to frighten or threaten the child into staying quiet. They will use the knowledge of the child to incite fear.

- Some of the activities include making the child feel that no one will believe them; telling the child that by saying something it will cause discord in the family; threatening someone in the child's family, i.e., mother, sibling, grandparent, etc; among other threats that cripple a child into silence.

After frightening the child into silence about the abuse, the molester will systematically take every opportunity to molest the child, completely eroding self-esteem or sense of self-value, further making it likely that the child will never talk. Eventually, believing they are at fault for continually trusting the perpetrator, the child assumes responsibility for the molestation. Parents, be reminded, you are the child's protection. Be sure you are constantly paying attention to who your child is around and how they respond to them.

NOTE: Be mindful that there are some parents who are also predators. These cases can be more difficult to identify and have much more detrimental impacts on the child's emotional and psychological development. All the strategies herein must be monitored even more in such circumstances.

Online Predator Strategy

According to The U.S. Department of Justice, 1 out of 7 children will receive unwanted sexual solicitations on the Internet by online predators; and 1 out of 25 children will be enticed to meet online predators in person. Every parent or guardian has to be consistently mindful and aware that any child who has access to technology is a potential target for online predators, and predators have become extremely proficient at getting to children online. Banning your child from social media, especially as they enter the teen years, is not the answer. They will likely just go underground and get a secret account through friends.

So, what do you do? Education and open communication is key. When it is a person you know, they take time to get to know you and your child. However, with the World Wide Web, they don't need to get to know you. They zone directly in on your child with lies and mistruths. They tell them what they want to hear in words. They befriend your child in the comfort of their own rooms while you might be in the living room oblivious to what's going on. You need to educate yourself into the strategies these monsters use.

The Online Predator Approach

❖ Online Predators learn everything they can about your child from social media. Unfortunately, children today naively post everything about personal lives, what they are going through, along with unique identifying information.

❖ They develop an online persona that matches your child's interests and age. They will generally post fake pictures and videos that convince your child that they are a kid too. For some girls – the lure of an older, more experienced male is used.

❖ They join online gaming (or Xbox Live), chat sites, and popular apps that kids use.

❖ They will 'friend' your child's friends in a ploy to earn instant credibility with your child. Kids tend to trust someone who shares acquaintances with people they know.

❖ They then 'friend' your child under the guise that they have friends in common.

❖ They start to develop a close bond online, capitalizing on the knowledge that your child has revealed about their problems, their issues, their insecurities.

  ▪ They start talking to your child about their real life.

  ▪ They let them vent about you and their friends. They make the child feel like no one else understands them as they do.

❖ They start by sharing innocent pictures back and forth; then slowly begin to send more risky, sexualized pictures, which are rarely real pictures of them. Eventually, they then encourage your child to do the same.

  ▪ Once the child is conned into sending nude or partially nude pictures, the predator will now threaten the child with sextortion, saying things like, "I will show your parents and friends the pictures you sent me if you don't send me another picture doing [fill in the gross blank]."

  ▪ Sometimes, they will instruct the child to do sexually explicit acts in front of a webcam. It is often recorded and used for further sextortion.

❖ Some online predators will then convince the child to meet in person, which can easily escalate to rape, kidnapping, or child trafficking.

Keep Your Child Safe Online

❖ The ultimate plan is to have an open relationship with your child about sex and potential predator behavior, which really should start at an early age.

- However, if that has not happened, there is no better time to open the door to communication than now.

❖ Talk to your child about the strategies online predators uses to trick kids.

❖ Teach them to be careful about how much personal information they post online, and not to share identifying information, i.e., phone numbers, addresses, birthmarks, or any info that a stranger can use to identify them.

❖ Teach them that online predators use fake pictures and videos to make people believe they are also young. They will often use pictures of their previous victims or get fake pictures that will interest the child based on what the child has already revealed.

❖ Let them know that just because someone is friends with one of their friends online – it doesn't mean that their friends know them in real life. Knowing someone online is completely different from in-person knowledge.

❖ Make sure all their social media profiles are marked private.

❖ Find out how best to monitor your child's social media activity. If you want to get a real clear assessment of the online threat, contact your local police department and have a chat with someone from the computer crimes or child exploitation units. They can provide you current statistics and information; and might be the best source to give you some guidance on how to monitor your child's social media platforms most effectively.

❖ If you become a friend on your child social media page, don't be naïve. Kids make secret accounts, pre-teens as well as teens. So, if you do not see many postings on the account you are following – dig deeper. Do not allow passwords on electronics that you pay for. They might not be happy, but this is what's needed to keep them safe.

❖ Have a family charging station in the kitchen and require that all electronics get 'checked' for the night. If you are paying the bill, you set the rules.

❖ For extra security, you can purchase products like the Family Friendly Wireless Router which can give you parental controls and let you know about your child's internet usage.

- You can set time limits, block websites and apps, get a weekly usage report, and stop internet access at the touch of a button. This extra expense will be an investment in your child's safety.

❖ Keep up with the abbreviations kids use online. They change often. So, this is where the critical communication strategy comes into play. Talk to your child often and listen to what they say about 'text talk.' The stronger your open communication foundation with your child, the more they will talk to you openly about everything. Believe it or not, your child wants to be able to talk to you about everything. You can either ensure that door is wide open or shut tight.

- Here are a couple of text acronyms about parents:
  - PAW or PRW – Parents are watching
  - PIR – Parents in room
  - POS – Parent over shoulder
  - P911 – Parent emergency
- Essential for parents to know:
  - (L)MIRL – (Let's) meet in real life
  - MYT – Meet You There
  - P&C – Private and Confidential

If you were ever one of those parents that believed your child should have their privacy, just in case you didn't know, those days are over! You need to talk to your child consistently about the state of the Internet. Check your child's phone on a regularly scheduled basis. Talk to them about why the check is necessary.

When there are news stories of missing children due to online predators, talk to your child about the story and ensure they understand the details. Not that you want to scare them senseless; but you really do want to scare them senseless. The goal is to get them to understand that it is not about you distrusting them, but online predators are unscrupulous. The strategies online molesters use to get to children are devious, and you can't stand the thought of them being hurt.

❖ Look for apps that you don't recognize. This means that you are going to need to know a little about the popular apps. There are many apps out there that are designed for private communication that kids might try to hide. You need to know.

❖ Skim through texts. Who are they talking to? Do you see one-way conversations? If so, chances are your child is deleting some of the conversation they may not want you to see. You need to talk to them about it.

❖ Be advised... you will likely be called the worst parent EVER. You will likely hear, *"None of my friend's parents do this,"* *"This is not fair,"* *"You are so over-protective!"* You are not being overprotective, and any diligent parent will be doing the same thing. Good parents do hard things that won't necessarily earn you brownie points, but will keep your child safe. And for that – it's worth your child's displeasure.

❖ Know the parents of your child's friends. When you know the parents of the children your child calls friends, talk to them. There is truly strength in numbers. If several of you are doing the same due diligence checks, it will send a strong message to the children; and be easier for you all as parents to stay on top of what is happening.

Signs of Abuse

Having been a child of molestation, I can testify that when a child is being abused, they truly do try to send every sign they can to tell somebody to 'Help me, please.' The problem is most parents are not as tuned in to their children as they could be and miss the signs. Those signs are always present, but sometimes they can be confused with other childhood stressors. So, you must be present when your child is talking to you, and you need to know your child well.

❖ *Direct Physical Signs*

Direct physical signs that a child is being sexually abused are not always common, but may include:

- Bruising on arms and legs, which may signify being held down or forced in certain positions.
- Unexplained marks, redness, or swelling around the mouth, genitals, or anus.
- Urinary tract infections or sexually transmitted diseases (STDs).
- Unusual vaginal or penile discharge are additional warning signs.

❖ *Indirect Physical Signs*

Child sexual abuse victims will most often exhibit indirect physical signs as their cry for help:

- Very common signs include anxiety, chronic stomach pain, and headaches.

- Emotional and behavioral signals to include "too perfect" behavior, withdrawal, fear, depression, unexplained anger, and rebellion.

- Use of alcohol or drugs at an early age as a response sign of the trauma.

- Resilient children may not outwardly exhibit serious consequences, whereas other children with the same experience may exhibit highly traumatized behaviors. Some victims do not display extreme emotional responses to abuse. Signs may be more subtle. This is when parents must be present and in-tune with their child and his or her behaviors.

- Nightmares and bedwetting when in conjunction with other symptoms. These could have other causes; so, if this is the only adverse symptom, it is unlikely to be caused by sexual abuse, but should be investigated to determine the cause.

- Falling grades or adverse educational impact. If your child has been a good student, then suddenly has difficulties, be vigilant to determine the cause. This is a common sign of some kind of dire emotional stressor.

- Extreme anger responses to include cruelty to animals, bullying, fire setting, runaway, and self-harm of any kind.

- One of the most telling signs that sexual abuse is occurring is sexual behavior and language that is not age-appropriate.

Child sexual abuse victims may exhibit a wide range of immediate, indirect reactions that vary both in magnitude and form. Whatever you do, don't dismiss any of these symptoms as 'just a part of childhood.' One or two of these signs or symptoms may be innocent and in no way associated with a detrimental trauma. However, the more of these signs you observe, the more you need to delve into what is going on with your child.

I went through numerous emotional roller-coaster rides trying to let someone know that I needed help. On one occasion, I was asked, "Is anything wrong?" I said no with my head down, and the answer was just accepted. That ready acceptance of my response made me angry and enforced the feeling of having little value. Your child will likely be too afraid, embarrassed, and ashamed to tell you anything verbally. As their advocate, it's your job to 'investigate' and dig until you get answers.

Consequences of Child Abuse

Emotional and mental health problems are often the first consequence and sign of a child who is the victim of sexual abuse. Children who are sexually abused are at significantly greater risk for symptoms related to stress (including post-traumatic stress), severe anxiety, clinical depression, and even suicide attempts. The following summarizes the severe consequences:

❖ Psychological problems that lead to substantial disruptions in normal development with lasting impacts that lead to dysfunction and distress well into adulthood.

❖ High-risk behaviors during adolescent development to include promiscuity, drug, and alcohol abuse.

- Studies support that child sexual abuse victims are three to four times more likely to abuse drugs and alcohol.
- Drug abuse is more common than alcohol abuse for adolescent victims.
- Age of onset for nonexperimental drug use was 14.4 years old for victims, compared to 15.1 years old for non-victimized children.
- Adolescents were 2 to 3 times more likely to have an alcohol dependence problem than nonvictims.

❖ Delinquency and criminal acts that often stem from substance abuse are more common in adolescents with a history of child sexual abuse.

- Sexually abused adolescents are at three to five times more risk of delinquency.

❖ Behavioral problems such as physical aggression and noncompliant actions frequently occur among sexually abused children and adolescents.

- They exhibit increased patterns of angry, irritable moods; argumentative, defiant behaviors; or vindictiveness.
- Emotional and behavioral difficulties can lead to higher rates of delinquency, poor school performance, and dropping out of school.
- Adolescents that reported victimization were more likely to be arrested than their non-abused peers.
- They tend to perform lower on psychometric tests, which measure cognitive ability, academic achievement, and memory assessments, which adds to the difficulties in academic challenges.

❖ The risk of teen pregnancy is much higher for girls with a history of child sexual abuse.

  ▪ The increased risk for pregnancy at a young age is likely due to more promiscuous behaviors as a consequence of learning sexualized activities too early.

  ▪ Abused girls are two times more likely to become teen mothers than their counterparts.

❖ Sexually abused children were nearly twice as likely to run away from home.

How to Keep Your Child Safe

❖ Talk to your child about Sex.

  ▪ The strongest weapon you have in the war to keep your child safe from any threat is open, honest communication. This is a foundation that should be laid as early as possible.

  ▪ Many discussions need to happen with your child before having the 'sex talk' with your child. You and your child should be comfortable talking about any situation or circumstance. This will make it easy for them to come to you when and if something happens that makes them uncomfortable or afraid.

  ▪ If you have not been focused on doing so before, it is never too late to begin to open the doors to communication.

❖ Don't depend on teaching 'Stranger Danger.'

  ▪ Most parents are good at teaching the concept of 'stranger danger' by cautioning children to watch out for strangers approaching them.

  ▪ However, teaching the message of 'stranger danger' is not enough when it comes to child predators.

- According to the National Institute of Justice, 90% of children who were sexually abused were victimized by **someone they know**. That means the molester will likely be someone that **you know and likely trust**.

- 'Stranger danger' does not impress upon your child what to do if the predator is a family member, family friend, community advocate, or neighbor. Your conversation with your child must go much deeper than warning your child about strangers.

❖ Teach your child that their body belongs to them.

- From a young age, children need to be taught, *"My body belongs to me."* There are several books out there, as well as numerous YouTube videos that can help you have these conversations with young children in a non-threatening way.

- Teaching a child that their body belongs to them lets your child know that when it comes to their body, there are some parts that most people should not see and that certain touches are not acceptable.

- When a child is encouraged to be in charge of something, it empowers them. Even for a young child, it gives them a 'voice' that will help them talk to you if something happens that you need to know.

❖ Good touch and bad touch.

- To go along with teaching "my body belongs to me," your child needs to know that there is a difference between good touch and bad touch.

- Teach them that they can tell the difference between good and bad touch because we all have been blessed with instincts that tell us if something does not feel right. Teach them to trust their instincts.

- For a young child, a good way to explain instincts is to tell them that it is a special superpower they have that can keep them safe.
  - Let them know that their superpower will reveal itself if they are ever around someone who makes them feel uncomfortable.
  - Explain to them how the superpower will tell them if something is not right by feeling queasy, nervous, worried, funny feeling in the stomach, etc. This will help them recognize and be aware of what instincts feel like.
- Let them know that as soon as their superpower tells them that something is wrong, they must try to get away from anyone who makes them feel uneasy, and tell you as soon as they can.

Be Present, Be Mindful, Be There

Many parents feel uncomfortable talking to their children about sex. They wrongly think that if they talk about the topic, the child will be more prone to want to experiment. This is not true!

❖ When you have frequent conversations about sex with your child and in your family dynamic, it becomes normal, comfortable, and empowering for everyone. They won't feel compelled to seek more information or experiment because you will have opened the door to open dialogue. However, if you are embarrassed and refuse to talk openly about sex, and they are abused or touched inappropriately, they will feel ashamed and prone to keep it a secret.

❖ It will be easier for the molester to maneuver them to believe they are at their fault or talking to you will cause family problems. This is what predators depend upon. However, when you lay a strong communication foundation with your child, the likelihood of someone taking advantage of them and causing them harm will be greatly minimized.

❖ The greatest warning to give to parents is that if your child is victimized, and you find out about it, don't blame the child! They are already in pain and hurting.

- Family therapists tell us that children, at some level, always blame themselves for the things that happen to them. So, any mild indication that an adult blames them for their pain makes it easier for them to internalize the pain as their fault. As a result, they are literally victimized a second time for something that was never their fault.

- Victim-blaming occurs when the victim of a crime is blamed for the crime that happened to them. This often occurs with children because parents or other responsible adults find it difficult to accept that they, the parent, was culpable for their child being victimized or that they lost total control of the situation.

- When a child is victimized a second time with being blamed for their pain, that sense of betrayal by a parent more devastating than the actual abuse. Children can heal from abuse with their parent's or guardian's trust and help. It is much more difficult to bounce back from feeling betrayed by someone who should love and take care of them. If you don't believe them or if you blame them for their pain, you will literally commit them to living a life of devastation. When a child is abused, the only person that is to blame for that abuse is the child predator. NEVER blame the child for their pain!

Chapter 11
Destiny Detractors – At School

True courage that leads to greatness is developed by surviving difficult times and overcoming challenging adversity."
Barbara De Angelis

A critical aspect of laying a strong positive development foundation for a child's success is ensuring that "Destiny Detractors" don't derail the potential they possess. Chapter 10 focused on two critical factors that a child may have to deal with at home, childhood poverty and child molestation. This chapter will focus on three detractors that can assault a child at school which can critically detract from a child's great potential: school bullying, teen dating violence, and negative peer pressure.

SCHOOL BULLYING

In 2014, the Centers for Disease Control, in collaboration with the Department of Education, released the first uniform definition of bullying. The concept is formally defined as "acts or words intended to intimidate or harass a person or cause physical harm to an individual's property." The definition acknowledges two modes and four types of bullying. The two modes of bullying include:

❖ Direct Bullying - This is bullying that occurs in the presence of a targeted individual.

❖ Indirect Bullying - Bullying that is not directly communicated to the targeted individual but is more underhanded, such as spreading rumors.

The *four types* of bullying include the following:

❖ Physical - efforts to cause or inflict physical harm to the targeted individual.

❖ Verbal - efforts to humiliate the targeted individual through demeaning words, in person or online.

❖ Relational - efforts to harm the reputation or relationships of the targeted individual.

❖ Damage to Property – doing harm to or destroying the targeted individual's property or personal belongings.

Bullying can happen in any number of places, contexts, or locations, to include online aka cyberbullying. Aggressive bullying can quickly become a criminal act, if not checked, such as extreme harassment or assault.

The Numbers Speak

❖ Approximately 1 in 4 students in the U.S. will be bullied, with most bullying occurring in Middle School.

▪ The most common bully actions in Middle School involve name-calling, teasing, spreading rumors or lies; pushing or shoving, hitting, slapping, or kicking; purposeful exclusion, threatening, stealing belongings, sexual comments, or gestures; cyber-bullying.

▪ Students report the following most common places within the school that bullying occurs include in the classroom, hallways, or lockers, in the cafeteria, in the gym or PE class, in bathrooms, or on school grounds.

❖ Although the incidents of bullying seem to be declining marginally, it is still the most prevalent and serious problem that occurs in the school environment.

204

❖ In one extensive study, 49% of children in grades 4 through 12 reported being bullied at school and 30.8% reported actually bullying others.

❖ 33% of students who reported being bullied at school indicated that they were bullied at least once or twice a month during the school year.

▪ Of that number, 13% were made fun of, called names, or insulted.

▪ 12% were the subject of rumors and detrimental remarks and comments.

▪ 5% were pushed, shoved, tripped, or spit on.

▪ 5% were purposefully excluded from activities.

❖ Although bullying affects both males and females equally, females suffer from bullying slightly more than males.

❖ Only 20 to 30% of bullied students will ever report the bullying to an adult.

❖ Other kids in the school environment can make a huge impact on bullying. Research supports that more than half of bullying situations (57%) ends with peer intervention. This indicates that positive peer influence makes a definite impact on the bullying paradigm.

❖ Students' traits that are most likely to be subject to bullying include physical appearance, race or ethnicity, disability, religion, sexual orientation, and perceived weaknesses.

Effects of Bullying

❖ Students who experience bullying are at increased risk for poor school adjustment, sleep difficulties, anxiety, and depression.

205

- Students who are both targets of bullying are who bully are at greater risk for mental health and behavior problems.

- Students who are bullied have negative self-images; have problems with long term relationships, to include with family and friends; and have problems with schoolwork.

- Students who are bullied are twice as likely as their non-bullied peers to experience negative health effects such as headaches and stomachaches on a regular basis.

- There is a strong correlation between bullying and suicide-related behaviors. However, bullying does not cause suicide; it is the associated factors such as depression and detrimental feelings that manifest as a result of the bullying.

Signs That Your Child Is Bullied

Constant bullying can lead to a child feeling isolated, rejected, depressed, or anxious. These negative feelings of despair can and have contributed to suicide or suicidal tendencies. It is critical for parents to be consistently mindful of any behaviors that might suggest your child could be a victim of bullying. Be advised that any of these signs could be indicative of other stressors that children find it difficult to deal with. However, the signs below have been most associated with school bullying:

- **Finding reasons to avoid school.**
  With younger children, they find reasons to stay home, as well as requests from the school nurse for early pick-up. You will often hear them complain of headaches and stomach aches, which are manifestations of stress and anxiety. Try to get them to talk about their aches and pains

in a non-confrontational way to get them talking. Older kids tend to skip school altogether. So, if you have suspicions, check with the school to ensure that they are not leaving home but not going to school.

❖ **A change in friendships.**

Changing their circle of friends, or no longer hanging with established friendship. This is particularly the case with adolescent and teen girls. This could indicate that bullying is taking place within the group.

❖ **Troubled sleeping at night.**

When a child is anxious about what might occur at school the next day, his or her sleep will generally be disrupted. They will have trouble falling asleep or toss and turn during the night. If you notice your child seeming tired when getting up in the mornings, this could indicate a stressor that disrupts their sleep that you need to question.

❖ **Intense or uncharacteristic emotional responses.**

Intense emotional reactions related to conversations about school could indicate high anxiety, which could be a sign of something negative happening in the school environment. For younger kids, this can be triggered by discussion of school in general. For older kids, it might be more discussion of social activities related to school.

❖ **Not wanting to interact with the family.**

One of the most obvious signs that something might be wrong is when a child's interaction with family members changes. If a child is not as talkative when they get home from school or if they go straight to their room, take time to find out why. Additionally, acting out against siblings as a release of internal anger could be a sign of being a long-time victim of bullying.

❖ **Obsession with or complete withdrawal from electronic devices.**

If a child is you online, one of two things might happen – they may become over-attached to their electronic devices, or they might completely withdraw from them. If it's the former, your child will become agitated if you limit their usage generally due to them wanting to constantly check to see if any more progressive negative things are being said about them. With the latter, they are afraid to know what more is being said about them. Either way, you must seek to open the lines of communication with you.

❖ **Torn or disheveled clothing and physical marks.**

Torn, ruined, or unkempt clothing; damaged belongings; along with physical scrapes or bruises when a child gets home from school are definitive signs of bullying. When asked about what happened, the child will not be able to provide any viable explanation. The best approach is to ask open-ended, non-threatening questions, such as, "what happened today at school?" and gauge the reaction.

❖ **A 'victim stance' posture.**

Children who lack the skill or confidence to stand up for themselves, often assume a 'victim stance' in their posture. The 'victim stance' is defined as walking with head down, rarely making eye contact, and being too insecure to speak up. Not only is this a sign of potential bullying, but it also makes them an open target to being bullied even more. If you notice this posture in your child, communication is key; and consider getting them involved in some activity to enhance their sense of confidence.

❖ **Self-Injury, Eating Disorders.**

For older kids, adolescents and teens, bullying can lead to

internalizing the pain through self-injury or eating disorders. Self-injury behaviors are actions of deliberate harm to one's own body to include cutting and burning.

Another negative coping mechanism for teens in distress situations includes eating disorders, the most common of which are anorexia nervosa, bulimia nervosa, and binge-eating. These serious consequences must be addressed as soon as parents observe any signs.

❖ **The 'new kid' syndrome.**

Students without strong support systems are at the highest risk for bullying. That means that new kids at school or transfer students who have obvious self-esteem issues can be at the top of the list for victimology. If your child is in either category, be proactive in helping your child get to know the neighborhood kids as well as school staff.

Whether, as a parent, you observe a few of the signs above, or you note several, it is imperative to respond as quickly as possible to find out what is causing these signs to manifest in your child.

Prevention Strategies

Studies also have supported that school bullying can be prevented or the negative effects minimized by assuring the following strategies:

❖ **Parental Communication.**

Parents must establish a strong foundation of communication with their child as early as possible; and keep the lines of communication open continuously, encouraging children to talk to them about anything. They should seek to ensure that children are confident in who they are, so they do not present a 'victim stance' in the school setting. Parents should talk to their children about school bullying to help them avoid being a victim while encouraging them to extend kindness to others who may be victimized. Explain that not all children grow have caring, loving parents and that sometimes those kids turn into bullies.

❖ **Encourage the 'Buddy Up' System.**

Encourage your child to use the buddy system at school. Bullies most often target loners. So, ensure you are helping your child understand how to connect to others if they are new to the school. If they are not new, they should connect in friendship before the school year starts, so they already have bonded relationships. Additionally, urge them to befriend someone that seems to be alone or have no friends. One person can make a huge difference in someone else's life by simply reaching out in friendship.

❖ **Prepare the SILT Response.**

Once you initiate the conversation of bullying with your child, complete the conversation by giving them guidance on how to respond if they become a victim, or if they witness bullying. One of the best strategies for bullying defense is to teach your child the **SILT** strategy:

- **S**ay No: The child should clearly tell the bully to **stop**. This is the most difficult of steps as it's at this point that the target lets the bully know that they will not be mistreated. Generally, this will require the child to feign courage when they might be scared. However, it's important for the child to verbally communicates to the bully with confidence to 'back off!'

- **I**gnore: The child should not react with fear. Again,

this might initially be difficult; but as a parent, teach them how to act confident, even when they don't feel it. Bullies thrive on the negative response to their bullying, to inciting fear and pain. It is important that the child put on the bravest face they can at that moment; and do not cry, wince, or show negative reactions.

- **Leave:** The child should walk away from the situation. They must walk away with confidence, and head held high. Tell them to think about something that makes them feel good or positive about themselves to help them overcome whatever fear they may feel as they walk away. They should not look back as they walk away, nor look sad or hurt. Doing that lets the bully know that they made the child feel bad, and they will continue to bully them.

- **Tell Someone:** It's critical to tell a trusted adult immediately. The bully may continue to pose a threat if the targeted child does not say something to someone who can intervene. The best scenario is that with the right trust foundation, your child will come to talk to you. It is critical that you build that trust foundation early and work continuously to keep communication open.

The **SILT** strategy is not a natural response strategy, so you will need to practice it with your child, even if you don't feel that they might be a potential target. You don't have to make it scary or distressing. Turn it into a play or a game. Just get your child comfortable with the process, which will also serve to help them be more confident overall.

❖ **Know the Signs.**

Review the section above that outlines the signs of bullying and learn to recognize them. Make sure you are 'present' when you or your child are together at home after school. Being present means not only are you in the same room, but you are watching how they interact, listening to what they say (and don't say), and you are responding to them where they are.

Educator Interventions

❖ The most helpful thing a teacher can do to deter bullying with the students they teach is to listen to the student if they come with a complaint.

❖ Don't dismiss any bullying complaint as 'boys being boys' or telling the student to 'suck it up.' That is not helpful and could lead to litigation if the child is hurt, and it is revealed that an educator knew and did nothing.

❖ If a student comes to you, pay attention, check with them often, and contact parents to discuss the situation and plan a strategy to redress. As an educator, you often see things in real-time that parents don't. This is truly one of those situations in which you, working with the parents, can change a life.

❖ If the target student reveals the bully's identity, check with the school counselor to ascertain how best to approach the bully and the bully's parents to address the behavior. Remember, it is likely that the bully is also a victim of bullying in some areas. That may likely be by a parent, a family member, or someone older who bullied them. Their bullying behavior is a cry for help in the only way they know-how.

❖ Educators (teachers and administrators) must never tell students to solve the problem themselves. This will do nothing to help resolve the issue and will only prolong a child's suffering.

❖ No one should EVER tell a student that the bullying is their fault, that they should act differently, to ignore it, or that they need to stop being a tattle tell. There have been situations in which teachers have made these comments to victims of bullying. A child must be able to trust that at school, a teacher is a safe zone, not a blame zone.

TEEN DATING VIOLENCE

Domestic violence is defined as the willful verbal intimidation, physical assault, sexual assault, battery, or other abusive behavior perpetrated by an intimate partner against another. In the United States, it is an epidemic affecting every community and every economic group, regardless of race, religion, nationality, or educational background. It is often accompanied by emotional abuse and controlling behavior that becomes a consistent pattern of behavior that results in physical injury, psychological trauma, and sometimes death of the victim.

Children who witness domestic violence in the home are the silent victims who suffer long term emotional, behavioral, and cognitive problems. They are at greater risk for poor school performance, depression, physical ailment, and numerous other negative problems and outcomes. By their teen years, both males and females are at increased risk for drug and alcohol use, suicidal thoughts, and disruptive conduct to include engaging in toxic relationship behaviors in dating situations, either as victims or abusers.

The Statistics Speak

It's a sad reality that abuse in dating relationships is common more among teens in the U.S. than we would like to acknowledge. The following support an alarming trend that most parents would not like to think about that must be cause for imminent concern:

❖ Unlike domestic violence in the homes, males and females equally report being teen dating violence victims.

❖ Nearly 1.5 million high school students nationwide experience physical abuse from a dating partner every year.

❖ 33% of teenager report having been in some kind of toxic relationship with 12% admitting to being physically abused.

❖ 1 in 10 high school students have been purposefully hit, slapped, or physically hurt by a boyfriend or girlfriend.

❖ 1 in 5 female high school students reported being physically or sexually abused by a dating partner.

❖ In a study of 8th and 9th graders, 25 % acknowledged being victims of dating violence, with 8% disclosing being sexually abused - that's teens in the age range of 13 – 14 years.

❖ Girls who reported that they had been sexually or physically abused were more than twice as likely as non-abused girls to smoke (26% versus 10%), drink (22% versus 12%), using illegal drugs (30% versus 13%), and binging (32 % versus 12%).

❖ Females, 15 - 20, reported at least one violent act during a dating relationship, 24% reported extremely violent, such as rape or the use of weapons against them.

214

❖ In a study of adolescent mothers, 12 - 18 years, 1 in 8 pregnant adolescents reported having been physically assaulted by the father of their baby during the preceding 12 months.

❖ 50 to 80 % percent of teens report knowing someone involved in a violent relationship.

❖ Most teens involved in a toxic relationship never tell anyone of their pain, primarily due to guilt and shame.

❖ 81% of parents believe teen dating violence is not an issue or admit they don't know if it's an issue. What a parent does not know can be an extreme detriment to a teen.

The Prevalence of Teen Abuse

In a national survey of more than 272,000 teens in 6th – 12th grade, less than 50% of girls feel good about themselves, putting them at greater risk of victimization to include teen dating violence or toxic relationships. When a child does not have self-esteem or positive self-value, it becomes very easy for them to be mistreated and suffer in silence. Toxic relationship behaviors fall into several categories. Below are the most practiced forms for teenage interactions:

❖ **Emotional Abuse**

Emotional abuse is often hard to recognize because it can be subtle and initially, it can seem like overly caring. As time progresses, the abuser chips away at self-esteem and the victim's self-worth, which leads to feelings of self-doubt, guilt, and some level of shame. The most common form of emotional abuse is verbal, which can begin subtly, then progresses to more aggressive interactions.

  ▪ Subtle Emotional Abuse:

- Ignoring or excluding the victim from activities.
- Isolating victim from friends, family, and social interactions.
- Subtle Humiliation in front of others.
- Sarcastic teasing and jokes.
- Slowly discouraging interactions with friends under the guise of spending time with the abuser.
- Making decisions for them without asking or obtaining permission.
- Making derogative or slanderous statements about an individual to others.
- Demeaning or criticizing the victim about dress, weight, makeup, or anything that undermines confidence.
- Being disrespectful in front of others.

- Aggressive Emotional Abuse:
  - Yelling or swearing at the victim.
  - Name-calling or insults.
  - Mocking the victim, generally for things they can't change about themselves.
  - Threats and intimidation, using something that the victim is not confident about.
  - Judging and criticizing the victim about areas they otherwise would feel proud of.
  - Blaming the victim for 'problems' that only the abuser identifies as problems.
  - Threats of violence or abandonment if the victim is no compliant to abuser's expectations.
  - Intentionally frightening the victim with threats to loved ones.
  - Aggressively ordering victim around, inciting fear and intimidation.

- Lying to the victim, or about the victim to others, in an effort to isolate.
- Making rules about what the victim can say, do, wear, whom to talk to.
- Exhibiting rage when things don't go the abuser's way; it's a reaction to them losing control over the victim.

❖ **Cultural/Spiritual Abuse**

- Attacking or ridiculing the victim's belief system or culture.
- Attempting to stop the victim from practicing or participating in spiritual practices.
- Attempting to use spirituality or religion as a means of controlling the victim.
- Destroying spiritual or cultural objects that the victim holds dear.
- Attempting to force the victim to accept spiritual beliefs or engage in spiritual practice that abuser prefers.

❖ **Cyber-Technology Abuse**

- Criticizing victim on social media by spreading rumors, lies or gossip.
- Monitoring victim's phone calls, emails, and texts to control behavior.
- Posting cruel photos or videos without victim's consent, to humiliate and hurt.
- Sending harassing texts, emails, and messages that threaten, intimidate, and terrify; even during the night to disrupt sleep and maximize negative impact.

- Recruiting friends, family members, and others to harass and intimidate victim via text, email, or social media.
- Using GPS and other online apps to track the victim's whereabouts.
- Setting up false accounts on social media sites to gain access to victim's information.
- Hacking into the victim's social media accounts and email to access info, post inappropriate things as the victim to get them in trouble.

❖ **Psychological Abuse**

- Exhibiting possessiveness and jealousy, under the guise of extreme love.
- Calling consistently to find out what the victim is doing and where they are, under the guise of being concerned with their welfare.
- Manipulating victims by making all the decisions.
- Threatening to kill themselves if the victim expresses a desire to end the relationship.
- Correcting victim under the guise of helping them.
- Leaving unwanted gifts, flowers, or other items with notes of threats.
- Withholding affection when abuser is upset.
- Stalking victims.

❖ **Physical Abuse**

- Slapping, hitting, kicking, biting, or punching.
- Scratching, strangling, choking.
- Pushing, pulling, grabbing, throwing, shoving.
- Throwing things at the victim.

- Pulling hair, snatching the arm, or yanking clothing to command obedience.
- Aggressively grabbing the victims face to make them look at the abuser to emphasize control.
- Causing bruises, cuts, broken bones, etc.
- Hurting those the victim loves, or violent threats to do so.
- Driving recklessly with the victim in the car.
- Using a gun, knife, box cutter, or other weapon to undergird a threat.

❖ **Sexualized Abuse**
- Emotionally pressuring victim to have sex when they don't want to.
- Forcing the victim to have sex or perform sexual acts.
- Emotionally pressuring or forcing the victim to have sex with other people.
- Demanding victim wears more (or less) provocative clothing.
- Forcing victim to engage in sexting; then threatening to expose details or photos.
- Making degrading sexual comments, especially in front of others to humiliate.
- Making threats if the victim doesn't comply with sex.
- Forcing victim to have sex for money or to participate in pornography.

Relationship abuse is all about control and manipulation. Since the teen brain is not fully developed in the teen years, most of the behavior an abuser exhibits will generally be learned behaviors. Emotional abuse is purposed to get the victim to depend upon and trust the abuser, while they are alienated from those who would otherwise be a support system. Psychological abuse gets the victim positioned to hold themselves accountable for the abuse that they experience.

Victims are made to believe that if something goes wrong or if the victim seeks to be free of the abuse, they will be the blame of any bad thing that happens to them, their family, or the abuser. The other forms of abuse are about control. Victims will need to have a strong support system to get out of the toxic relationship. They are not responsible for anyone's actions but their own. As parents, you will need to help them climb the ladder to a place of empowerment.

Warning Signs of Teen Dating Violence

Going through some moodiness is just part of the growing process for a teenager. However, sudden or drastic changes in behavior, attitude, or demeanor is generally an indication that something needs to be addressed, such as a potentially

unhealthy relationship. This is one of the many reasons that, as a parent, you must know and consistently communicate with your child. If you suspect your child might be in a toxic relationship, below are some behaviors that might be warning signs to look forward:

❖ Failing grades or an unusual disinterest in classes.

❖ Dropping out of school activities, which were once of targeted interest.

❖ Avoiding or pulling away from friends or their social circles.

❖ Difficulty making decisions when it never seemed to be a problem in the past.

❖ Sudden changes in mood, attitude, or personality, acting out, exhibiting signs of anxiety or depression, being secretive, or noncommunicative.

❖ Having bruises, scratches, or other injuries with lame or unlikely explanations.

❖ Changes in eating or sleeping habits.

❖ Avoiding eye contact with you or other family members, with obvious signs of pulling away from family activities.

❖ Constantly making references to the 'dating partner,' including obsessing on what he or she might think.

❖ Using drug, alcohol, or other negative coping mechanisms.

❖ Becoming pregnant - some teens believe that having a baby will help make the situation better, or some are forced to have sex against their will resulting in an unwanted pregnancy. Although this alone does not indicate dating violence, combined with other signs, it could be an indication.

❖ You notice that the person your child is dating is jealous or possessive of your child, especially when they have conversations with individuals of the opposite sex.

❖ The 'dating partner' gets angry when your child talks to or hangs out with their friends.

❖ The 'dating partner' seems to have a lot of control over your child, to include their decision making and actions.

Healthy Relationships Defined

It is critically important to understand what a toxic relationship is and how to avoid one. It is just as crucial to understand what a healthy relationship is and what that term really means. Many individuals have no clue what a healthy relationship looks like, and some don't feel they deserve a healthy relationship. If your child has been exposed to any toxic behaviors in the home, they may now believe that the toxic behavior is normal. You will now need to help them redefine what 'normal' looks life.

Helping your teen understand what a healthy relationship looks like and how they should be valued in a healthy relationship will help them set their own standards for what they will and will not accept in a dating situation. Your message will help them set those standards high. But remember, the loudest message is the example you set for them on a daily basis. Psychologist, Dr. Doug Haddad, supports that three critical components define a healthy relationship: communication, compromise, and caring.

❖ **Communication**: In a healthy relationship, each partner is comfortable and empowered to be who they are and feel comfortable expressing their thoughts and feelings. They don't operate in fear, respectfully speaking their minds. They embrace opportunities to talk openly, and because of the level of respect for each other, they actually enjoy talking to each other.

❖ **Compromise**: In every relationship, there will be times of disagreement. In healthy relationships, partners don't fear disagreeing with each other. Each acknowledges that their partner's voice matters and has value. They focus not on the differences to build contention but seek to find common ground to find solutions to problems in a peaceful, respectful manner. They share decision-making with a foundation of trust in each other.

❖ **Care**: To care for someone means respecting the individual enough to be compassionate, patient, and supportive. It means when one partner has problems, concerns, or issues; the other partner is available to help any way possible to get to resolution; employing empathy in seeking to understand what the partner is going through. It is building each other up rather than tearing each other down. Caring for someone means that you will generally put that person's needs ahead of one's own.

All three components work together to create a healthy relationship. Have an open discussion with your teen about healthy versus toxic relationships. Remember, the best example is the life you are exposing them to.

Parental Interventions

The best way to protect your child from teen dating violence, as with any other threat to their vast potential, is your intervention as a parent. The following strategies are steps you can take to protect your child:

❖ Emphasize the importance of not engaging in sex at an early age, maintaining an abstinent lifestyle. Research supports that the earlier a teen engages in sexual activity, the greater the threat of getting trapped in a toxic relationship.

❖ Stay alert, pay attention, be present for your child. It's critical that you are always alert and pay attention to what is going on with your child. Take an active interest in the individuals your child is dating. Insist on meeting them, and occasionally, invite them to activities whereby you can see how they interact with your child. Pay attention to any signs of abuse as outlined in this chapter.

❖ Talk to your child early about dating, relationships, and sexual behavior. This is part of the open and honest communication between parent and child that is so critical. Don't assume that if you don't talk about it, it won't happen. Unfortunately, that is the very reason that so many teens are long term victims. Let your teen know they can talk to you about any issue at any time. Look for opportunities in your discussions to give examples of and reinforce messages of empowerment and self-value. Believe it or not, teens are always listening, even if it seems they have tuned you out ☺ . Be an active listener, ensuring that you are listening more than you talk. You will be surprised they are willing to share if they know you will hear them and not judge them.

❖ Provide a 'safe place' for your child to be able to talk to you about their problems. When they come to you with serious issues, don't over-react, and under no circumstances do you give them the impression that anything is their fault. Find out the facts, and work with them to get out of harm's way.

❖ Be an example for your child. The most telling scene that signifies the likelihood of a child being a victim or a perpetrator is what they see at home. Don't just tell them about having healthy relationships; show them what healthy relationships look like. If you are married and have marital issues, your child should not see continuous contention, aggression, or violence. If you need help making that happen, get it. Call your pastor, a counselor, or a professional who can help you master positive coping mechanisms. If you are single, be careful who you bring in your home, and what your child sees as interactions.

❖ Monitor your child's social media accounts and activity. Most teenagers live in the confines of their social media presence. Not a lot that goes on with them won't be mentioned on social media. As discussed in the previous chapter, you need to have access to your child's social media and their phones. They may get upset with you at first, but it's a cross you just need to bear.

❖ Know the social media platforms that your teen uses and create your own accounts in those platforms. Being active on social media will give you a good look at your teen's life. It will also keep you relevant on what's going on in the social media world. If you are one of those parents who dislike social media and online activities, get over it! You are your child's strongest advocate. You can't be an advocate if you don't know what's going on.

❖ Be someone who your teen can relate to. Many teens don't talk to parents because parents erroneously think they must be seen as perfect. None of us are. Your teen needs to know that you have made mistakes, have learned from them, and want to do as much as you can to help them not fall into the pits that you fell in to. It's especially good to let them know if you have faced some of the same challenges that they might bring to you. Give them specific examples of when you stumbled and fell, and the struggles of getting back up. This will make you relevant to what they are going through, and they will hang on to you for any help they need. Remember…they want to talk to you. You need to give them a reason to do so.

Raising a teen is no easy task in today's society, with so many things competing for your child's attention. As your child's advocate for their safety and success, you must trust your instincts and act on them for the good of your child. No one knows your child better than you do. Be present in their lives and stay on alert. You can be the shield that protects them from abuse.

PEER PRESSURE

A child is, without a doubt, a parent's most valuable treasure; at least, that's what should be the case. It is imperative that you invest the time and effort needed to give them all that is needed to position them for success. However, the wise parent knows that they are not a child's only influence. The older they get, the more outside influences seek to monopolize your child's time. They are their own individuals, and your goal must be to eventually get them to a place of making their own decisions. By being mindful of the reality that outside influences can interfere with the message you plant within them, you need to understand what peer pressure is and how to deal with it.

Understand Peer Pressure

Peers are individuals who are included in the same social group or who have a shared focus. The term 'peer pressure' is defined by Merriam and Webster as "feeling that one must do the same things as other people of one's age and social group in order to be liked or respected by them." In other words, it's the perceived influence that members of the peer group have on each other.

The concept of peer pressure is not necessarily negative. However, the term 'pressure' implies that the result of the influence will result in someone doing things they would not otherwise choose to do or that the action may not be the wisest route to take. As a result, the perception of 'peer pressure' is that peers influence members to indulge in behaviors that are not socially desirable or acceptable. The concept of 'peer pressure' is generally not associated with positive peer influences.

Parents must understand the impact of peer pressure and not underestimate how influential it can be in a child's life. Only by coming to terms with the huge effect of peer pressure on a child can parents help children maneuver through the maze and manage peer pressure outcomes. Below are some fundamental facts about peer pressure:

❖ There are two driving types of peer pressure: implicit and explicit.

- Explicit peer pressure results from external sources, whereby members of the peer group place pressure on the child to do or behave a certain way. Explicit pressure may be members threatening to expel a child from the group if they do not join in going to a party where kids are drinking when it is against what a parent has instructed.

- Implicit peer pressure is the internal pressure children place upon themselves as a result of how they process what goes on around them. Implicit pressure may be a situation in which a child dresses one way on the first day of school, then comes home and ask the parent if they can purchase a different style because their current attire does not fit the style that their peers are wearing; and they want to fit in.

- Parents need to understand the difference between the two types, so they can meet their child where they are when peer pressure concerns arise.

❖ Peer pressure influences brain development in teens. Research studies have found that peer pressure influences the parts of the brain that are involved in risk and reward, which seem to have a direct link to the presence of peers:

- Adolescence generally begins around age 12. However, you may notice adolescent changes as early as 8 years old for girls, and 9 years old for boys. This is another critical reason that, as a parent, you need to communicate with and know what's going on with your child.

- Adolescent youth brain development is characterized by a drive to seek unique experiences and engage in impulsive risk-taking behaviors. This is part of the growth process in identifying their individuality.

- The adolescent tendency to engage in high-risk or dangerous behaviors is attributed to the underdevelopment of the prefrontal cortex, the part of the brain that controls decision-making, planning, and reasoning.

- Adolescents have a much stronger desire and need for peer acceptance than younger children or adults. As a result, the concept of peer pressure is more of a threat when a child hits the adolescent years and beyond. There is a strong desire to be accepted by their peer group, to 'fit in,' and not be excluded, all of which can trigger insecurities, self-doubt, and hurt.

- Adolescent risk-taking behaviors are heightened in the presence of peers, as evidenced by the occurrences of reckless driving, engaging in criminal activities, and drug and alcohol abuse. These incidences occur with much more frequency with other adolescents or are generally as a result of peer influence.

- Recent studies support that adolescent decision-making is directly influenced by the mere presence of other adolescents, and that they took significantly more risks when observed by their peers. Translation: they sometimes do unwise things when they are with their peers.

- These research findings mean that adolescent youth are more likely to engage in risky behavior when they are with friends, compared to when they are on their own. As parents, we must take this into consideration when providing information and guidance on managing peer pressure.

❖ Peer pressure is a fact of adolescent life; parents need to prepare every child to deal with it. Your child will have to deal with peer pressure at some point in their teen years. There is no way to protect children from it, short of keep them isolated in a bubble at home. So, your best strategy is to prepare them to deal with it, so that you can be confident that they will make the best decisions possible when you are not around.

Peer Pressure Preparation

So, as a parent, how do you prepare your child to deal with peer pressure?

❖ Establish a strong foundation of open communication.

- A major factor in guiding your child through the forces that shape them at school is open, honest, and consistent communication. As a parent, you have a lot of influence over your child; and your voice is constantly with them when they are not in your presence. Although it may not seem that way to you, your influence is greater than any other influence in your child's life. However, for your influence to speak over other voices, you must instill a strong foundation of self-value, and they know they can come to you for anything.

- You do not have to be overbearing or give them the impression you don't trust them. You just need to establish a foundation whereby they trust you and know that you are there for them without judgment, whatever the situation. Sit down with then to ask about their day, what they experienced, and if there were any issues, they want to discuss with you. Be present, listen intently, and observe non-verbal communication while you listen. When you get to a foundation of trust, there won't be too much they won't share with you.

❖ Discuss your expectations and emphasize your desired value system.

- It is important for your discussion to include clear communications related to your desires for their safety and success. Establish a strong foundation for what you would like to see related to behaviors. The key is to make sure you and the household is living up to the value system you expect of your child. That means the discussions of expectations should begin long before you have the peer pressure discussion. If that has not happened, start from where you are with a family discussion of what is desired as your family values going forward. It will be a long journey to develop the trust foundation. However, with consistency and continuous communication of the message, your child will embrace your influence.

- Be sure that the rules and expectations are reasonable; and that you clearly communicate what is acceptable, what is unacceptable, and what should be avoided. The more you impress the message, the more your child will be guided by an intrinsic knowledge of what to do if they find themselves in situations that counter the value expectations of you and the household.

- What you instill in and teach your child is the intrinsic blueprint that they will mentally consult when faced with difficult situations, not only in school but throughout their lives. As a parent, it is your duty to ensure that they know what they should and should not do in order to be healthy, empowered, successful individuals. If an adolescent feels confident, secure, and loved, they will be less likely to choose to hang with risk-oriented peers or indulge in risky behaviors.

❖ Be involved, be present, and stay connected.

- Be sure that you are there for your child. Being present is different from just having a conversation at dinner time. It means shutting out the noise of your day and giving your child your undivided attention, one child at a time. It means that if they need your assistance, you are there to give them what they need. It means that they fully understand and believe that they are your first priority.

231

- This also means that you make time to do things outside of the home whenever possible to include attending parent-teacher events, going to their events, and functions at school and in the community. It means that you take time to participate in their interest areas and get to know their friends.

- These actions tell your child that they matter to you; that no matter what happens that you will be there for them. If this message resonates with them, your voice and the power of your influence will be a protective shield when they are faced with decisions related to peer pressure.

❖ Maintain a safe, trusting in-home environment.

- Studies support that adolescents and teens who have a strong, trusting relationship with their parents are more likely to resist peer pressure. It's important to keep an open mind in all conversations and refrain from judgmental responses. It is quite likely that at some point, your child will make a mistake in some area. When they do, talk to them with care and concern rather than criticism.

- Talk to them about why the decision was not a great decision, the impact, and consequences of the decision, and what can be learned to ensure the mistake does not reoccur. Include them in what needs to be done to deal with the issue so that everyone can move forward.

- Be sure that as you help them understand the detriment of the decision, you also reinforce the message of your love, support, and that the mistake does not define who they are.

❖ Although most discussions of peer pressure are about negative outcomes, keep in mind that not all peer pressure is bad. When peer pressure influences your child to do something positive, like stepping out of a comfort zone, learning something new, or experiencing something positive, it should be embraced as a growing experience for your child. Only by having open discussions with your child will you know how to manage the peer pressure discussions.

The Peer Pressure Communication

When having the peer pressure conversations with your child, there are several key points you need to emphasize. Highlight the following points:

❖ **Healthy friendships don't make you feel bad about you.**

Let them know that *real* friends won't make them feel bad about them or their decisions; real friends will accept them for who they are without judgment. Real friends will never make them 'prove' themselves to be called a friend. You can help them assess their friendships by asking them, *"how does (friend's name) make you feel?"* This question can help them reach their own conclusion about the friendship.

❖ **They should trust their instincts.**

Tell your child to use their internal alarm system to guide them if a person, situation, or decision is good for them. Explain that if they have a funny feeling in their gut or what some call 'that icky feeling,' that is generally their instinct telling them it is likely not a good decision. They need to learn to trust their instincts when it comes to friends and decisions.

❖ **Learn to understand how to make healthy choices.**

Emphasize that your child has the power to make decisions

related to who they choose to hang with and what they choose to do. No one can force them to do something unless they are being threatened with hurt or harm. Help your child to understand the pros and cons of participating in negative behaviors, such as attending a party with alcohol, using drugs, joy riding, etc. Have a real, frank discussion with real outcomes, so they understand the dangers.

❖ **Be empowered to say 'no.'**

Saying 'no' is a lot harder than it sounds, especially for adolescents and teens who are most often asked to make 'in the moment' decisions. Have discussions with your child ahead of time on how to say 'no' in a way they feel most comfortable. This is how to help them get out of a situation when the easiest thing to do is say 'yes.'

- The critical component of this point is to help your child understand that you believe in their ability to make good decisions, and they must be confident in their decision making. Help them see the difference in saying 'no' with confidence verses saying 'no' timidly.

- It might be a good idea to role-play so they can visually see how body language must align with what's coming out of their mouth when they say 'no.' Set up several adolescent and teen situations and scenarios and walk through the best 'no' strategy. Have them act out how they would respond if they were asked to go to a party where there will be alcohol without adult supervision? How would they handle it if someone asked to cheat off their test? How would they respond if a female friend asked them to go with them to meet someone from an online connection?

- Depending on your child's personality, humor can ease the discomfort of a situation. For instance, they might say: "No, thanks. I'm seeking social outcast status 😊."

❖ **Tell them to always stay true to who they are.**
  - Statistics support that there are likely others in the peer group who also want to say no, but may not have the confidence to do so. When your child can remain true to who they are, they can be the model for positive behavior and lead others down a more positive path. When they stay true to themselves, there will be no guilt, shame, or other negative after-effects to deal with. They will be able to stand in confidence in what is right for them.

Giving your child the tools to be empowered in their decision-making, and being confident in who they are is the best support you can give them to position them for long term success. When you arm them with the right information, you enhance their potential to live healthy, productive, happy lives while attaching to healthy, supportive relationships.

CHAPTER 12
Wisdom for Parental Success

Don't let yourself become so concerned with raising a good kid that you forget that you already have one." Glennon Melton-Doyle

Parents and other caregivers play a critical role in ensuring a child's educational success, which is the foundation for life-long achievements. A common misconception that many parents have is that teachers and the school staff wield the greatest influence on a child's learning capacity. Such could not be further from the truth. Although teachers do have significant influence on a child's educational journey, the most powerful influence in a child's life in education, as well as every other area of importance, is a child's parent.

It's Never Too Late

Research supports that what happens at home, before kindergarten, is the most emphatic path to set a child on the path of educational success. However, if as a parent, you are getting a late start in engaging in your child's journey, know that it is never too late to influence your child. You owe it to them to help them embrace the importance of learning and education to life-long success.

One of the most fundamental ways to do that is to just start interacting with your child on a fun level. An easy way to kick off the journey to emphasize learning is to start is with books. If your child is younger, identify a character they like and read to them. If they are older, focus on a topic of interest to them and have them read to you, or read together. If it's a teen, read about something that they are interested in, share your ideas about what you read; then ask them for their input.

Reading to and with your child is one of the most important ways to emphasize how important you think learning is to their success. It is the best way to infuse family fun in the learning journey, and an easy way to express your expectations of your child in preparing for success without making it sound like a threat. Reading has amazing benefits to your child as well as to you and your family unit.

For the child at any age, it builds strong literacy skills, strengthens cognitive capacity, stimulates the imagination, invigorates the creative part of the brain, improves listening skills, and expands verbal aptitude. For you as the reader or participant in reading with your child benefits you by reducing your stress levels, helps you relax, improves your concentration even when it's child level books, and helps bond with your child. The simple, inexpensive strategy of reading helps infuse the joy of learning in your child and opens up their concept of possibilities.

Another easy win in building the right framework for your child's educational success is to understand the importance of building healthy, secure relationships with your child. Again, if this was not done before, it is never too late to start. A child is always yearning for a very close connection to their parents or those who are their primary caregivers. They are also very forgiving of mistakes when the parent lets them know they want more closeness and engagement as a parent. Just let them know they are loved more than they can know. Apologize for any past issues that may have led to them thinking otherwise. A healthy, secure attachment to you as a parent builds confidence, self-esteem and helps them believe in their potential to be successful.

Remember that children learn best through their everyday experiences and interactions with the people they love and trust. These interactions serve as modeling behaviors for a child's mental and emotional development. This is especially true of a parent, a child's primary role model, who literally provides the foundation of how a child sees their capacity to learn, grow, and be all that they can be.

How you interact, what you say, how you say it, how you react to them, and what you don't say to them – all impact of how they see themselves and what they feel they can achieve. No matter what age, you begin to build the right foundation by bonding and engaging positively with your child. Through this level of engagement, they will instinctively begin to have more confidence, establish a healthy sense of self, and feel more secure in their capacity to be successful.

Begin the Bonding Journey

The powerful impact of parents and caregiver interactions on a child's concept of their capabilities is unquestionable. So how do you begin the journey to lay the right foundation to bond with your child or get closer to your child, especially if you have not done so in the past? Some quick steps to begin the journey are as follows:

❖ The impact of touch is powerful on the human spirit, even more so when that healthy touch is between parent and child. Hug your child when they walk in the room, when they come home from school, when they share any news they have to share. Your simple hug tells them that you are there for them, you love them, and you are always in their corner.

238

❖ End their day with a loving gesture. For younger children, tuck them in bed with a kiss and a bedtime story. For older children, even teens, hug them, tell them you love them (you can never say that too much), and wish them a good and restful night's sleep.

❖ Never be too busy for them. After school, take 15 minutes or so to ask them about their day and listen to what they say without judgment. This is just as important for older ones (including teenagers) as it is for the elementary ages.

❖ For younger children, make running errands an educational experience by engaging children with dialogue. Have them describe sites as you drive; in the store take about unusual items. Anything can be a topic to engage them. What you talk about is not important. Engaging them is key.

❖ For older children, listen to what's going on in the world. Ask the child, especially teens, what they think or how they feel about the issue. Listen to their points of view; show them you respect their thoughts. This strategy is one of the best ways to help your teen understands that they are valued, that what they think matters, and that their voice is one to be heard.

❖ Play with your child, young and older. Show them you know how to have fun; and that you enjoy having fun with them. Laugh with them. Watch television together. Have at least one meal during the day together and share the day's activities and events.

❖ Don't let the limitations of your circumstances undermine your relationship with your child. Poverty and lack of financial means can be difficult and make it harder for parents to participate in school activities. However, that does not take away from your ability as a parent to hug, love, and show your child how much you support them and are proud of them. They need that more than they need you to participate in activities.

There will be so many opportunities to engage with your child, bond with them, tell them how proud you are to be their parent, and show them you believe in them. Parenting is not a passive role. Be on the alert to take every opportunity to show your child how much you care about and support them. Remember, your child does not need a perfect parent; they just need a loving one!

Inspirational Quotes for Parental Engagement:

Below are some powerful inspirational quotes concerning parenting and the critical importance of your parenting role. Read each quote carefully so that you fully understand what the quote is saying and how it impacts you as a parent on your child's life journey. Anything that resonates in your spirit, write it down, commit it to memory. Let the quote inspire you in those times you feel you want to lose it ☺. Happy Parenting!

❖ Don't worry that children never listen to you; worry that they're always watching you. *Robert Fulghum*

❖ You, the parent, are your child's first teacher and their best teacher. It's an awesome responsibility, but one that brings immeasurable rewards. *Jacquie McTaggart*

❖ Parents with their words, attitudes, and actions possess the ability to bless or curse the identities of their children. *Craig Hill*

❖ The truth is that the perfect mom/perfect child concept is a myth. The only perfect parent is God, and you ain't Him. *Cheri Fuller*

240

❖ The golden rule of parenting is to always show your children the kind of person you want them to be. Remember that children are impressionable. *Elizabeth Roxas*

❖ It was vitally important to a child's development that you model the behavior that you want your child to adopt. As a parent or parental figure, you have a tremendous responsibility that should not be taken lightly. *Catherine Pulsifer*

❖ If there is anything that you wish to change in your child, you must first examine to see whether it is not something that you must address and change in yourself. *C.G. Jung*

❖ Parents are not perfect, nor are they saints. Dads and moms make mistakes all the time. How you handle those situations will be a critical life lesson for your children. *Bethany Bridges*

❖ My father gave me the greatest gift 1 human can give another. He believed in me! *Jim Valvano*

❖ I may not be able to give my kids everything they want, but I can give them everything they need: love, time, and attention. You can't buy those things. *Nishan Panwar*

❖ When you truly realize who gave you your child, why you do what you do and how you do what you do will totally change as you understand that none of this is about you and what you think and feel. It's all about the purpose and plan that God has for that child's life. *Joseph Woodley*

As a parent, your child needs you to be their number one, very vocal advocate on their journey in life. They need your patience and tolerance; they need your commitment; they need your dedication; they need your understanding. They need you to be there when no one else is. They need you to believe in them when no one else does. They need you to help them understand and embrace why school, education, and life-long learning is so important to their life-long success. They need you to help position them to succeed in all they do, and to know that your belief in them is unwavering.

By meeting their needs, you will help position them to achieve the greatness that God created them to achieve. If you are not the unwavering, loving advocate they need, they won't be able to be all that they were born to be. No matter the circumstance or situation, your child needs you to help unleash their educational excellence, in school and life, so they can soar into the phenomenal individuals they are meant to be. Make every moment you have with them count!

Parental Assistance Checklist

Show the Importance of Education and Homework

➤ Do you set a regular time every day for homework?

➤ Does your child have the papers, books, pencils, and other things needed to do assignments?

➤ Does your child have a fairly quiet place to study with lots of light?

➤ Do you emphasize interest by talking to your child, asking questions, and following up each day?

➤ Do you set a good example for your child by reading and writing yourself?

➤ Do you set an example by letting your child see you pursuing your own goals to improve and better yourself?

➢ Do you stay in touch with your child's teachers, not only when problems arise, but throughout the school year?

Monitor Assignments

➢ Do you know what your child's homework assignments are? You don't have to understand them in order to make sure that they are doing the assignments.

➢ How long should they take? This requires communication with your child's teacher.

➢ How does the teacher want you to be involved?

➢ Do you ensure that assignments are started and completed on time?

➢ Do you read the teacher's comments on assignments that are returned?

➢ Is TV viewing cutting into your child's homework time?

Provide Guidance

➢ Do you understand and respect your child's style of learning?

➢ Does he or she work better alone or with someone else?

➢ Does he or she learn best when they see things, hear them, or handle them?

➢ Do you help your child to get organized?

➢ Does your child need a calendar or assignment book to get organized?

➢ Do you encourage your child to develop good study habits (e.g., scheduling enough time for big assignments, making up practice tests)?

> Do you talk with your child about homework assignments?

> Does he or she understand the assigned work?

Talk With Someone Concerning Problems

> Do you meet the teacher early in the year before any problems arise?

> If a problem comes up, do you meet with the teacher with an open mind?

> Do you cooperate with the teacher and your child to work out a plan and a schedule to fix homework problems?

> Do you follow up with the teacher and with your child to make sure the plan is working?

To every parent, whether in the home, non-resident father, foster parent, and / or parenting a special needs child ...your every word, every action, and every reaction matters. Every positive action you don't take matters. You job is to nurture the seed of greatness in your child to promote sequoia growth for destiny and purpose. You can't afford to fail. Make your role count!

May you and your child have a phenomenal learning and educational journey!

ACADEMIC
&
FAMILY
SUPPORT
RESOURCES

Educational Support Organizations / Resources

ERIC Clearinghouse on Disabilities and Gifted Education
1920 Association Drive
Reston, VA 22091
Toll Free: 1–800–328–0272
http://www.ericec.org/

ERIC Clearinghouse-Elementary and Early Childhood Education
The National Parent Information Network (NPIN) / Children's University of Illinois at Urbana-Champaign, Research Center
51 Gerty Drive
Champaign, IL 61820–7469
Toll Free: 1–800–583–4135
ERIC/EECE: www.ericeece.org / http://www.npin.org

Nat'l Information Ctr-Children & Youth with Disabilities
P.O. Box 1492
Washington, DC 20013–1492
Toll Free: 1–800–695–0285 (voice & TTY)
http://www.nichcy.org

National Institute for Literacy (NIFL)
800 Connecticut Avenue NW, Ste. Suite 200
Washington, DC 20006
Toll Free: 1–800–228–8813
http://www.nifl.gov

Nat'l Institute Early Childhood Development & Education
U.S. Department of Education
Office of Educational Research and Improvement
555 New Jersey Avenue NW
Washington, DC 20208
Phone: 202–219–1935
http://www.ed.gov/offices/OERI/ECI/

U.S. Department of Education
400 Maryland Ave., SW

Washington, DC 20202
Phone: 202–205–5465
http://www.ed.gov/offices/OSERS

No Child Left Behind
Parents Tool Box
U.S. Department of Education
Toll Free: 1–888–814–NCLB
http://www.nochildleftbehind.gov/parents/index.html

Office of Special Education and Rehabilitative Services
U.S. Department of Education
400 Maryland Avenue, SW
Washington, D.C. 20202
1-800-872-5327
https://www2.ed.gov/about/offices/list/osers/index.html

Foster Care Support Organizations

Casey Family Programs
2001 Eighth Avenue, Suite 2700
Seattle, WA 98121
Phone: 206-282-7300
https://www.casey.org
Casey Family Programs provide research and expertise on laws and policies to better the lives of children in foster care and their families.

Child Welfare League of America
727 15th Street, NW, 12th Floor
Washington, DC 20005
Phone: 202-688-4200
Email: cwla@cwla.org
CWLA leads and engages its network of public and private agencies to advance policies and strategies to help vulnerable children, youth, and families.

Children's Bureau
330 C Street, S.W.
Washington, D.C. 20201
www.acf.hhs.gov
As the oldest federal agency within the Administration for Children and Families, the Children's Bureau is responsibility for administering federal child welfare programs.

Children's Defense Fund
25 E Street NW
Washington, D.C. 20001
Phone: 800-CDF-1200 (800-233-1200)
Email: cdfinfo@childrensdefense.org
www.childrensdefense.org
CDF is a child advocacy organization to help lift children out of poverty; protect them from abuse and neglect; and ensure access to health care, quality education, and a spiritual foundation.

Foster Care Alumni of America
5810 Kingstowne Center Dr., Ste. 120-730
Alexandria, VA. 22315

248

Phone: 918-862-2586
Email: info@fostercarealumni.org
https://fostercarealumni.org/
FCAA is a national non-profit association founded to connect the foster care alumni community and to transform foster care policy and practice.

Foster Care Network
1-800-4-KIDS-27
info@fostercarenetwork.org
http://www.fostercarenetwork.org
The FCN is the leading "match-maker" for foster children, helping "match" loving families with dedicated foster care agencies to place youth in care.

Foster Club
810 Broadway Ave., Ste 203
Seaside, OR. 97138
Phone: 503-717-1552
Email: info@fosterclub.com
https://www.fosterclub.com
Foster Club is a national network to promote opportunities for youth in foster care to connect with each other and help them realize their full potential.

Jim Casey Youth Opportunities Initiative
701 St. Paul Street
Baltimore, MD 21202
Phone: 410.547.6600
http://www.aecf.org
The Casey Initiative works to ensure that young people, ages 14 and 25, make successful transitions from foster care to adulthood.

National Foster Parent Association
1102 Prairie Ridge Trail
Pflugerville, TX. 78660
Phone: 800-557-5238
Email: Info@NFPAonline.org
http://nfpaonline.org/
NFPA is a non-profit, volunteer organization established to support foster parents in achieving safety, permanence, and well-being for youth in their care.

249

Special Needs Support Organizations

Council for Exceptional Children
2900 Chrystal Drive, Suite 100
Arlington, VA 22202
Phone: 888-232-7733 / TTY: 866-915-5000
https://www.cec.sped.org
The largest international professional organization dedicated to improving the educational success of children with disabilities.

Easter Seal
141 W Jackson Blvd., Suite 1400A
Chicago, IL 60604
Phone: 800-221-6827
http://www.easterseals.com/
Easter Seals provides opportunities for people of all ages with a range of disabilities to achieve their full potential.

Family Voices
P.O. Box 37188
Albuquerque, NM 87176
Phone: 505-872-4774 / 888-835-5669
http://www.familyvoices.org
Family Voices "aims to achieve family-centered care" for all special needs children by providing families with the "tools to make informed decisions".

Federation for Children with Special Needs
529 Main Street, Suite 1M3
Boston, MA 02129
Phone: 617-236-7210 / 800-331-0688
https://fwww.csn.org
This national organization promotes the active and informed participation of parents of special needs children in shaping and influencing public policies.

Friendship Circle International
816 Eastern Parkway
Brooklyn, NY 11213
Phone: 718-713-3062
http://www.friendshipcircle.com

The organization brings together teenage volunteers and children with special needs for hours of fun and friendship.

Goodwill Industries International
15810 Indianola Drive
Rockville, MD 20855
(800) GOODWILL
contactus@goodwill.org
http://www.goodwill.org
GII is a non-profit organization that provides job training, employment placement, and other community-based programs for people with special needs.

National Collaborative on Workforce & Disability for Youth
4301 Connecticut Avenue, NW, Suite 100
Washington, DC 20008
Phone: 877-871-0744 / TTY: 877-871-0665
http://www.ncwd-youth.info
NCWD helps young teens to learn to cope with their disability, identify employment options, and access educational opportunities.

Nat'l Dissemination Center for Children with Disabilities
35 Halsey St., 4th Floor
Newark, NJ 07102`
Phone: 973-642-8100
http://www.parentcenterhub.org/nichcy-gone
NDCCD provides a repository of information, programs, and services on youth with disabilities and special needs.

National Parent Technical Assistance Center
https://www.parentcenternetwork.org
The NPTAC provides resources and materials about special needs children to community centers and families in areas all around the country.

National Youth Leadership Network
https://nyln.org/
Led by young citizens, NYLN works to build strength and "break isolation" among people with disabilities between the ages of 16 and 28.

Parent to Parent USA
1825 K St, NW, Suite 250
Washington, DC 20006
Phone: 855-238-8979 / 518-637-9441
http://www.p2pusa.org/
This group matches parents with a buddy parent who has a child with the same disability, to provide parent to parent emotional support.

Special Needs Alliance
7739 E. Broadway Blvd. #362
Tucson, AZ 85710
Phone: 877-572-8472
https://www.specialneedsalliance.org
The SNA is a cohort of attorneys dedicated to the practice of disability and public benefits law, serving individuals with disabilities and their families.

Special Olympics
1133 19th Street NW
Washington, DC 20036
Phone: 202 628-3630 / 800 700-8585
https://www.specialolympics.org
Through the power of sports, SO provides people with intellectual disabilities the opportunity to discover new strengths, abilities, skills and success. .

The ARC
1825 K Street, NW, Suite 1200
Washington, DC 20006
Phone: 800-433-5255
https://www.thearc.org
The Arc is the nation's leading advocate, providing services for people with intellectual and developmental disabilities and their families.

The M.O.R.G.A.N. Project
4241 N. Highway 1.
Melbourne, FL 32935
Phone: 321-506-2707
http://themorganproject.org/
Making Opportunities Reality Granting Assistance Nationwide supports families in their journey of raising a special needs child, including foster care.

252

BIBLIOGRAPHY

AboutKidsHealth (2017). *Letters for Your Child's School.* Retrieved from http://www.aboutkidshealth.ca/En/HealthAZ/ TestsAndTreatments/ Complex-Care/Pages/letters-for-your-childs-school.aspx

Ackard, D., Neumark-Sztainer, D., Story, M., & Perry, C. (2007). Parent-child connectedness and behavioral and emotional health among adolescents. *American Journal of Preventive Medicine, 30,* 59-66.

Albert D. & Steinberg L. (2011). *Peer influences on adolescent risk behavior.* Springer Publishing, New York, NY.

Allen, S., & Hawkins, A. (1999). Maternal gatekeeping: Mothers' beliefs and behaviors that inhibit greater father involvement in family work. *Journal of Marriage and the Family,* 61 (1), 199-212.

Alwin, D, & Thornton, A. (1984). Family origins and the schooling process: Early versus late influence of parental characteristics. *American Sociological Review,* 49, 784-802.

American Academy of Child and Adolescent Psychiatry (2016). *School Services for Children with Special Needs: Know Your Rights.* Retrieved from https://www.aacap.org/aacap/families_and_youth/facts_for_families/F FF-Guide/Services-In-School-For-Children-With-Special-Needs-What-Parents-Need-To-Know-083.aspx.

American Federation of Teachers (2001). *Helping Your Child Succeed: How Parents & Families Can Communicate Better with Teachers and School Staff.* Washington, DC. Retrieved from http://www.aft.org/parentpage/communicating/index.html.

Anderson, A. L. (2002). Individual and contextual influences on delinquency: The role of the single parent family. *Journal of Criminal Justice,* 30 (6), 575-587.

Amato, P. (1994). Father-Child Relations, Mother-Child Relations, and Offspring Psychological Well-Being in Early Adulthood. *Journal of Marriage and the Family* 56(4): 1031-1042.

Beautrais, A. (2003). Suicide and serious suicide attempts in youth: A multiple group comparison study. *American Journal of Psychiatry,* 160, 1093-1099.

Bernadette-Shapiro, S., Ehrensaft, D., & Shapiro, J. (1996). Father participation in childcare and the development of empathy in sons: An empirical study. *Family Therapy*, 23 (2), 77-93.

Blair, C., & Raver, C. (2012). Child development in the context of adversity. *American Psychology*, 67(4), 309–318.

Blakemore, S. (2008). The social brain in adolescence. *Nature Reviews Neuroscience*, 9, 267–277.

Blanes, C. (2017). *Is homework a waste of time?*, 48-49. Retrieved from https://search.proquest.com/docview/1906105466? accountid=458

Boyse, K. (2009). *A guide to managing television: Tips for your family*. University of Michigan Health System.

Brannigan, A., Gemmell, W., Pevalin, D. J., & Wade, T. J. (2002). Self-control and social control in childhood misconduct and aggression: The role of family structure, hyperactivity, and hostile parenting. *Canadian Journal of Criminology*, April, 119-142.

Bronte-Tinkew, J., Moore, K. A., & Carrano, J. (2006). The father-child relationship, parenting styles, and adolescent risk behaviors in intact families. *Journal of Family Issues*, 27 (6), 850 – 881.

Brown, B. & Bakken, J. (2011). Parenting and peer relationships: Reinvigorating research on family-peer linkages in adolescence. *Journal of Research on Adolescence*, 21(1), 53–165.

Brown, L. (2007). Adolescent dating violence: The perspectives of a researcher and a parent. *The Brown University Child and Adolescent Behavior Letter*, 23(11).

Busy Kids Happy Moms (2016). *Top 10 conference tips for parents*. Retrieved from https://www.busykidshappymom.org /conference-tips.

Cabrera, N., Tamis-Lemonda, C., Bradley, R., Hofferth, S., & Lamb, M. (2000). Fatherhood in the 21st Century. *Child Development*, 71, 127-136.

Carlson, M. J. (2006). Family structure, father involvement, and adolescent behavioral outcomes. *Journal of Marriage and Family*, 68, 137-154.

254

Census Bureau (2016). *2015 Annual social and economic supplement, Table POV01.* Retrieved from https://www.census.gov/ programs-surveys/cps.html.

Center for Disease Control, National Center for Injury Prevention and Control (2015). Understanding bullying. Retrieved from https://www.cdc.gov/violenceprevention /pdf/bullying_factsheet.pdf

Cherlin, A. (1992). *Marriage, divorce, remarriage.* Harvard University Press, Cambridge, MA.

Christian, S. (2002). Supporting and retaining foster parents. *National Conference of State Legislatures State Legislative Report,* 7, 11.

Clark, R., Hawkins, D. & Vachon, B. (1999). *The school-savvy parent: 365 insider tips to help you help your child.* Free Spirit Publishing, Minneapolis, MN.

Close, S. (2005). Dating violence prevention in middle school and high school youth. *Journal of Child and Adolescent Psychiatric NurSing,* 18(1),2-9.

Code of Federal Regulations, Title 45, Subtitle B, Chapter XIII. *Foster Care Maintenance,* Subchapter G, Part 1356.

Colorín Colorado (2009). *Twenty ways you can help your children succeed at school.* Retrieved from http://www.colorincolorado.org/ article/twenty-ways-you-can-help-your-children-succeed-school.

Coley, R. L., & Medeiros, B. L. (2007). Reciprocal longitudinal relations between nonresident father involvement and adolescent delinquency. *Child Development,* 78 (1), 132-147.

Cook, E., Buehler, C.. & Fletcher, A. (2012). A process model of parenting and adolescents' friendship competence. *Social Development,* 21(3),461–481.

Côté, S., Lopes, P., Salovey, P., & Miners, C. (2010). Emotional intelligence and leadership emergence in small groups. *The Leadership Quarterly, 21*(3), 496-508.

Crone, E. & Dahl, R. (2012). Understanding adolescence as a period of social-affective engagement and goal flexibility. *Nature Reviews Neuroscience,* 13, 636–650.

Crowe, M., Ward, N., Dunnachie, B., & Roberts, M. (2006). Characteristics of adolescent depression. *International Journal of Mental Health Nursing, 15,* 10-18.

DataBank Trends (2016). Food insecurity: Indicators of child and youth well-being. Retrieved from https://www.childtrends.org/wpcontent/uploads/2016/12/117_Food_I nsecurity-1.pdf. 3Coleman-Jensen,

DeGarmo, J. (2012). *Fostering love: One foster parent's journey.* CrossBooks Publishing, Bloomington, IN.

Department of Health and Human Services (2016). *The maternal, infant and early childhood home visiting program: Partnering with parents to help children succeed.* Retrieved from http://mchb. hrsa.gov/programs/homevisiting/programbrief.pdf. 8U.S.

Dishion, T., Bullock, B., & Granic I. (2002). Pragmatism in modeling peer influence: Dynamics, outcomes, and change processes. *Development and Psychopathology,* 14(4), 969–981.

Dolin, A. (2010). *Homework made simple: Tips, tools, and solutions to stress free homework.* Washington DC: Advantage Books.

Duhigg C. (2012). *The power of habit: Why we do what we do in life and business.* Random House Publishing, New York, NY.

Dunkle, J. (2010). *Dealing with the behavioral and psychological problems of students: A contemporary update.* New Directions for Student Services #128. Jossey-Bass Publishing.

Evans, G., & Schamberg, M. (2009). Childhood poverty, chronic stress, and adult working memory. *Proceedings of the National Academy of Sciences of the United States of America,* 106(13), 6545–6549.

Fagan, J., & Barnett, M. (2003). The relationship between maternal gatekeeping, paternal competence, mothers' attitudes about the father role, and father involvement. *Journal of Family Issues,* 24 (8), 1020-1043.

Festinger, T. (1999). The foster care crisis: Translating research into policy and practice. *Television Viewing and School Achievement, Journal of Communication,* 34(2), 104-118.

Flouri, E. (2005). *Fathering and child outcomes.* John Wiley & Sons Ltd, West Sussex, England.

Formoso, D., Gonzales, N., Barrera, M., & Dumka, L. (2007). Interparental relations, maternal employment, and fathering in Mexican American families. *Journal of Marriage and Family,* 69, 26-39.

Freeman, C. (1996). *Living with a work in progress: A parents' guide to surviving adolescence.* National Middle School Association.

Gallopin, C., & Leigh, L. (2009). Teen perceptions of dating violence, help-seeking, and the role of schools. *The Prevention Researcher,* 16(1), 17-20.

Garber, S., Garber, M. & Spizman, R. (1993). *Good behavior.* Villiard Books, New York.

Gardner, M. & Steinberg, L. (2005). Peer influence on risk taking, risk preference, and risky decision making in adolescence and adulthood: An experimental study. *Developmental Psychology,* 41, 625–635.

Garey, J. (2018). *The benefits of watching TV with young children.* The Child Mind Institute. Retrieved from https://childmind.org/ article/benefits-watching-tv-young-children.

Gini, G. & Espelage, D. (2014) Peer victimization, cyberbullying, and suicide risk in children and adolescents. *JAMA Pediatrics,* 312, 545-546.

Goleman, D. (2012). *Emotional intelligence: Why it can matter more than IQ (Ed.10).* Bantam Books, New York, NY.

Grayson, J. (2006). Maltreatment and its effects on early brain development. *Virginia Child Protection Newsletter,* 77(37), 1-16.

Greenfeld, L. (1997). *Sex offenses and offenders: An analysis of data on rape and sexual assault.* U.S. Department of Justice, Office of Justice Programs, Bureau of Justice Statistics, NCJ-163392

Gurland, G. (2016). *How to advocate successfully for your child: What every parent should know about special education law.* CreateSpace Independent Publishing Platform.

Grych, J. H., & Fincham, F. D. (1990). Marital conflict and children's adjustment: A cognitive conceptual framework. *Psychological Bulletin*, 108, 267-290.

Harris, K.M., and Marmer, J.K. (1996). Poverty, paternal involvement, and adolescent well-being. *Journal of Family Issues* 17(5): 614-640.

Hawkins, D., Pepler, D., & Craig, W. (2001). Naturalistic observations of peer interventions in bullying. *Social Development*, 10(4), 512-527.

Henderson, A., & Berla, N. (1994). *A new generation of evidence: The family is critical to student achievement*. Columbia, MD: National Committee for Citizens in Education.

Herman, J. (2009). There's a fine line ... adolescent dating violence and prevention. *Pediatric Nursing*, 35(3), 164-170.

Holcomb, J. & Holcomb, L. (2015). *God made all of me: A book to help children protect their bodies*. New Growth Press, Greensboro, NC.

Howard, D., Wang, M., & Yan, F. (2007). Psychosocial factors associated with reports of physical dating violence among U.S. adolescent females. *Adolescence*, 42(166),311-324.

Jeglic, E., & Calkins, C. (2018). *Protecting your child from sexual abuse: What you need to know to keep your kids safe*. Skyhorse Publishing, New York, NY.

Jensen, E. (2013). How Poverty Affects Classroom Engagement. *Educational Leadership*, 70(8), 24-30.

Jeynes, W. (2007). The relationship between parental involvement and urban secondary school student academic achievement: A meta-analysis. *Urban Education*, 42(1), 82-110.

Lamb, M.E. (1997). *The role of the father in child development (3rd Ed)*. John Wiley & Sons, Inc., New York, NY.

Leeb, R., Lewis, T., & Zolotor, A. (2011). A review of physical and mental health consequences of child abuse and neglect and implications for practice. *American Journal of Lifestyle Medicine*, 5(5), 454-468.

Lips, D. (2007). *Foster care is failing*. USA Today, Vol 136.

Liu, J., Zhao, S., Chen, X., Falk, E., & Albarracín, D. (2017). The influence of peer behavior as a function of social and cultural closeness: A meta-analysis of normative influence on adolescent smoking initiation and continuation. *Psychological Bulletin,* 143(10), 1082-1115.

Markham, L. (2012). *Peaceful parent, happy kids: How to stop yelling and start connecting (The peaceful parent series).* The Penguine Group, New York, NY.

Marsiglio, W. (1991). Paternal engagement activities with minor children. *Journal of Marriage and the Family,* 53(4): 973-986.

McLanahan, S., and Sandefur, G. (1997). *Growing up with a single parent: what hurts, what helps.* Harvard University Press, Cambridge, MA.

McWilliam, R. (2010). *Routines-based early intervention: Supporting young children and their families (Ed.1).* Brookes Publishing, Baltimore, MD.

Milletich, R., Kelley M., Doane, A., Pearson, M. (2010). Exposure to interparental violence and childhood physical and emotional abuse as related to physical aggression in undergraduate dating relationships. *Journal of Family Violence,* 25(7), 627–637.

Mischel, W., Shoda, Y. , & Peake, P. (1988). The nature of adolescent competencies predicted by preschool delay of gratification. *Journal of Personality and Social Psychology,* 54, 687-696.

Myers, R. (2011). The Importance of a regular routine to your child. *Child Development Institute.* Retrieved from https://childdevelopmentinfo.com/ authors/robert-myers-phd.

Myers, R. (2015). A quick guide to understanding your child. *Child Development Institute.* Retrieved: https://childdevelopmentinfo.com / child-development/understanding-your-child-guide.

Nathanson, A. (2012). *Watch TV with your kids, but…* Psychology Today.

National Center for Education Statistics (2016). *Indicators of school crime and safety: 2015 U.S. Department of Education.* Retrieved from https://nces.ed.gov/fastfacts/display.asp?id=719

National Conference of State Legislators (2013). The Forum for America's Ideas. *Educating Children in Foster Care.* Washington, D.C.

National Dissemination Center for Children with Disabilities (2002). *Communication with your child's school through letters.* Academy for Educational Development, Washington, D.C.

Office of the President of the United States (2015). *Long-term benefits of the supplemental nutrition assistance program.* Retrieved from https://obamawhitehouse.archives.gov/sites/ obamawhitehouse. archives.gov/files/documents/SNAP_report_ final..

Olafson, E. (2011). Child sexual abuse: Demography, impact, and interventions. *Journal of Child & Adolescent Trauma,* 4(1), 8-21.

Patchin, J. & Hinduja, S. (2016). Summary of our cyberbullying research (2004-2016). *Cyberbullying Research Center.*

Pecora, N., Murray, J., & Wartella, E. (2006). *Children and television: Fifty years of research* (Routledge Communication Series). Laurence Erlbaum Associates, Mahway, NJ.

Polanin, J., Espelage, D., & Pigott, T. (2012). A meta-analysis of school-based bullying prevention programs' effects on bystander intervention behavior and empathy attitude. *School Psychology Review,* 41(1).

Ramey, S. & Ramey, C. (1999). *Going to school: How to help your child succeed: A handbook for parents of children 3 to 8.* Goddard Press, New York, NY.

Reed, K., Nugent, W., & Cooper, R. (2015). Testing a path model of relationships between gender, age, and bullying victimization and violent behavior, substance abuse, depression, suicidal ideation, and suicide attempts in adolescents. *Children and Youth Services Review,* 55, 125-137.

Riley, R. (1994). *Helping children to succeed: schools and parents must work together.* New York: USA Today, 123, 68.

Rose, C., & Espelage, L. (2012). Risk and protective factors associated with the bullying involvement of students with emotional and behavioral disorders. *Behavioral Disorders,* 37, 133–148.

Sedlak, A., Mettenburg, J., Basena, M., Petta, I., McPherson, K., Greene, A., & Li, S. (2010). *Fourth national incidence study of child abuse and neglect (NIS–4): Report to congress, executive summary.* U.S. Department of Health and Human Services, Administration for Children and Families, Washington, DC.

Shimmin, S. & White, H. (2006). *Every day a good day: Establishing routines in your early years setting*. Paul Chapman Publishing, London.

Shonkoff, J.P. (2010). Building a new bi-developmental framework guide to the future of early childhood policy. *Child Development*, 81, 357-376.

Signe Anderson, C., Hayes, C. & Rosso, R. (2017). Hunger doesn't take a vacation: Summer nutrition status report. *Food Research and Action Center*. Retrieved from http://www.frac.org/wp-content/uploads/2017-summer-nutritionreport-1.pdf. 13U.S.

Southard, J. (2019). *Fun In first: A teaching blog*. Retrieved from https://funinfirst.com.

Spear, L. (2000). The adolescent brain and age-related behavioral manifestations. *Neuroscience & Biobehavioral Reviews*, 24, 417–463.

Spilt, J., Hughes, J., Wu, J., & Kwok, O. (2012). Child development, dynamics of teacher-student relationships. *Child Development, 83*(4), 1180–1195.

Theriot, M. (2008). Conceptual and methodological considerations for assessment and prevention of adolescent dating violence and stalking at school. *Children & Schools*, 30(4), 223-233.

Toner, J. & Freeland, C. (2016). *Depression: A teen's guide to survive and thrive*. Magination Press, Washington, DC.

Tough, P. (2016). *Helping Children Succeed: What Works and Why*. Houghton Mifflin Harcourt. New York, NY.

Townsend, C., & Rheingold, A. (2013). *Estimating a child sexual abuse prevalence rate for practitioners*. Darkness to Light, Charleston, S.C.

U.S. Department of Education. (1994). *Strong families, strong schools: Building community partnerships for learning*. Washington, DC: Author.

U.S. Department of Education. (2002). *Helping your child with homework*. Washington, DC. Retrieved from http://www.nochildleftbehind.gov.

U.S. Department of Education. (2002). *Homework tips for parents.* Washington, DC. Retrieved from http://www.nclb.gov/parents/ homework/index.html.

U.S. Department of Education (2018). *Special education guide: The IEP process explained.* Retrieved from https://www.special educationguide.com /pre-k-12/individualized-education-programs-iep/the-iep-process-explained.

U.S Department of Health and Human Services Administration for Child Welfare: *Foster Care Statistics.* Retrieved from www.childwelfare.gov

Vaziri Flais, S. (2018). Caring for your school-age child (3rd Ed.). *American Academy of Pediatrics.* Penguin Random House, New York, NY.

Wolfe, D., Wekerle, c., Scott, K., Straatman, A., & Grasley, C. (2004). Predicting abuse in adolescent dating relationships over 1 year: The role of child maltreatment and trauma. *Journal of Abnormal Psychology,* 113(3),406-415.

Wright, P. & Wright, P. (2006). *From Emotions to Advocacy: The Special Education Survival Guide (2nd Edition).* Harbor House Law Press, Hartfield, VA.

This publication is designed to provide practical information regarding the subject matter covered. It is sold with the understanding that the author does not purport to render legal, counseling, or other professional advice. If legal advice or other professional assistance is required, the services of a competent professional should be sought.

Feel free to send feedback to:
Dr. Brenetia Adams-Robinson
drbre@epitomexcel.com

Made in the USA
Middletown, DE
09 September 2024

60083469R00156